The Angels of God

The
Angels of God
Understanding the Bible

by
Judith Lang

New City Press

London Dublin Edinburgh
New York Manila

Published in the United States, Great Britain, and the Philippines by
New City Press, 202 Cardinal Rd., Hyde Park, NY 12538
New City, 57 Twyford Ave., London W3 9PZ and
New City 4800 Valenzuela St., Sta Mesa, 1016 Manila
©1997 Judith Lang

Cover design by Nick Cianfarani

Library of Congress Cataloging-in-Publication Data:

Lang, Judith, 1939-
    The angels of God : understanding the Bible / Judith Lang.
    p. cm.
    Includes bibliographical references.
    ISBN 1-56548-101-1
    1. Angels. 2. Angles—Biblical teaching. I. Title.
BT966.2.L25   1997
235'.3—DC21   97-30286

Scripture quotations, unless otherwise indicated, are used
with permission from The Revised Standard Version

Printed in Canada

Contents

Personal Acknowledgements

I am indebted to Professor A. K. Thorlby and Professor D. F. Pocock for great help and encouragement at different stages of writing this book; also many other friends who have taken interest, and looked at parts of the manuscript from time to time.

Acknowlededgments

Permission has been granted by the following copyright holders for quotations from the works listed:

Cassell Ltd. *The Catechism of The Catholic Church* (1994) John F. C. Powys. T. F. Powys, *Mr Weston's Good Wine* (1927) The Rev. Timothy Radcliffe OP. Cornelius Ernst, 'How to See an Angel.' in F. Kerr and T. Radcliffe ed. *Multiple Echo* (1979) and T. Radcliffe, 'As one who Serves.' in *The Tablet*, 11.7.92.

Faber and Faber. T. S. Eliot, 'Ash Wednesday' in *Complete Poems and Plays* (1969). W. H. Auden, 'For the Time Being' in *Collected Longer Poems* (1968). S. Heaney, 'Markings' and 'Crossings' in *Seeing Things*. (1991) D. Jones, *The Anathemata* (1952).

Peter Levi. 'The Fox-coloured Pheasant enjoyed his Peace' in *The Gravel Ponds*, Andre Deutsch (1960).

Gabriel Josipovici. *The Book of God*. Yale. (1988)

Gerard Casey. 'The Shield of Achilles' in *Echoes*, Rigby & Lewis (1990) and Mary Casey, 'A Meditation on Angels' in *The Clear Shadow*, Rigby & Lewis (1992).

Burns & Oates Ltd. J. A. Jungmann, *The Mass of the Roman Rite* (1959)

Oxford University Press. W. H. Longridge, *The Spiritual Exercises of Ignatius Loyola* (1922). G. Keynes (ed.), *Blake; Complete Writings* (1972).

Canon A. M. Allchin. *The Furnace and the Fountain* (Cardiff 1987).

Random House U.K. Ltd. Annie Dillard, *Pilgrim at Tinker Creek*, Jonathan Cape Ltd (1975).

Thomas Merton Legacy Trust. Thomas Merton, *The Sign of Jonas* (1953).

Redeem the unread vision in the higher dream

(T. S. ELIOT, *Ash Wednesday*)

Introduction

What are angels? Do they really exist? There are no certain answers to either question. Many people scarcely ask the first, because of their doubts about the second. They think of angels as figures of fantasy, literary inventions and artistic decoration. They may recognize that angels appear in nearly all religious traditions, but do not give much consideration to them as a reality. Even committed believers may leave the subject aside, never examining their own thoughts about it. Iconography has been unhelpful in some ways. The conventional depiction of angels as humans with wings strains credibility, though the best pictures will inspire some wonder, even awe, at what is being represented. The same applies to writings about angels; the profoundest force us to read between the lines.

The Christian Church teaches that angels are creatures made by God. Its doctrines are based chiefly on the Bible, enlarged by later writings and thought, and drawing on rich traditions in Judaism and other sources. There can be nothing hard and fast in these teachings; interpretation of the texts and discussion of theories and experiences uncover endless possibilities. Tradition should not be taken as a set of formulas; what is transmitted, handed on, is a living vision that can move with us into the future. An exploration into the bases of the Christian traditions about angels can perhaps clarify otherwise vague ideas as to what those traditions are, and how they relate to the present day.

Ultimately the existence of angels, like the existence of God, can be acknowledged only in faith. There is much to be learned, however, by reading, thinking, and remaining open to the experiences of other ages. This book is concerned mainly with what the Bible says about angels, and takes a fresh look at the texts in which angels figure. It is hoped that discussion of these texts, and other relevant writings, will throw light on this mysterious subject. Images fixed by familiarity may take on new life, and ancient stories speak to us of still living possibilities. There are undoubtedly people who are conscious of some higher potential near at hand, and for whom angels remain a real possibility. They experience communion with a spiritual realm that both is part of this world and leads beyond it. Some would express this as a perception of angelic action, others make less specific accounts. A great number of people have said they have actually seen angels, and there is a growing interest in angels at present, evident in the arts and theological discussion. Nostalgia – 'something to be recovered, a forgotten beauty, a kingdom'[1] – is combined with immediate experience, the availability of spiritual power here and now. Angels are here to help us, say the believers.

Even a sceptic may be prepared to consider 'what angels are' in terms of what is meant by the word *angel*, and this makes a useful starting-point. If we try to reach beyond the definitions of any particular tradition, we may say that the word *angel* indicates a being of spiritual power, a spirit in the service of some supremely high Spirit. Generally such spirits are not themselves gods; their superhuman nature is dependent upon the Divine for whom they perform special tasks or functions. This may be regarded as the most general concept conveyed by the word *angel*. Later in the book I shall discuss the specific title of 'angel' which was given to such spirits in the Judaic tradition.

Angels in the world traditions

In most religions the Divine is understood to delegate power to lower spirits who act with a certain amount of freedom. These spirits are not all good. Many writings describe conflict between the good or obedient spirits and a malevolent opposition. Ancient Persian mythology, for example, finds expression in the Zoroastrian scriptures, the Avesta. There Ahura Mazda, the Lord of Wisdom, has a group of seven *amasha spentas*, or holy spirits, who work for him in specific ways. Acting against them is the spirit Angra Mainyu, who brings evil upon the world. There are also innumerable *fravashi*, winged spirits who inhabit the air; these appear to be spirits of the dead, assisting their own families and descendants.[2] Again, angels figure frequently in the Koran, the scripture of Islam which takes its origins from Judaism and other traditions further east. The disciples of Muhammad describe how Muhammad was visited by the angel Gabriel who told him, 'Recite, recite in the name of the Lord.' (The word *koran*, or *qu'ran*, means 'recital'.) Muhammad was later taken by an angel on a night journey; from Mecca he ascended with the angel towards heaven (*Koran*, Sura 17). The Koran proclaims that Muhammad, the prophet, is blessed 'by God and his angels' (Sura 33:56). There are also lesser spirits, *jinns*, who are capricious and may take possession of people; 'mankind and jinn, you will be judged' (Sura 55:26).

One further example may be mentioned: anthropologists working with African tribes find a consciousness of active spiritual powers. Professor Evans-Pritchard's study of the religion of the Nuer people of the southern Sudan describes how for them the one Spirit, or God, bears relation to lesser spirits at work on earth and in the sky. The Nuer appear to believe that the Spirit itself, whose home is 'in the sky', is at the same time immanent, in varying degrees, in persons, animals and things. It engenders the spirits whose life and movements are known by signs, given in many modes and on different levels of human experience. Particular conjunctions of natural phenomena can be read as signs of spiritual presence, and some creatures are considered to be manifestations of spirits with special functions. Birds are much respected as special symbols of spirit; they are in communication with God in the sky.[3]

These few examples are given to show the presence, in differing beliefs, of spiritual beings quite similar in their functions and characteristics to Judaeo-Christian angels. Whatever capacity or need it is in human beings that impels them towards religious belief appears quite regularly to cause them to relate not only to an ultimate reality or power or being, but also to lesser, intermediary manifestations of that Ultimate. We have only to note that the human mind in its search for some truth, or order, that transcends the ever changing and dying present has somehow found it necessary to formulate different orders of spiritual presence. Angels are one of these orders within Judaeo-Christian religious awareness, and they deserve our renewed attention at a time when so much emphasis is being placed on the social relevance and this-worldly presence of the Church. For it appears that the purpose of these spiritual powers is both to minister to life on earth, and to lead humankind towards knowledge of God and of our promised immortal life, by mediating between the human spirit and the pure and eternal Spirit of God. Awareness of the ministry and mediation of angels will awaken a new awareness of the full potential of our human nature.

Angels in the Christian tradition

My discussion will henceforth concentrate on specifically Christian awareness. It is important to be clear about differences, as well as similarities, between religions and religious traditions, because the lines which divide them form parameters, indicating unique approaches to God. Broad and generalized forms of understanding are not the same as religious belief. The individual believer makes a personal stake on one particular revelation of God, or risks wandering around on the wide and easy way described by Christ as the opposite to the 'narrow gate' (Matt. 7:13). The Christian way to God is through Jesus Christ, so it is through him that we will find greater understanding of what, in the Christian tradition, is meant by 'the angels of God'.

> Christ is the centre of the angelic world. They are *his* angels: 'When the Son of Man comes in glory and all the angels with him . . .' (Matt. 25:31). They belong to him

13

because they were created through him and for him: 'For in him all things were created in heaven and on earth, visible and invisible, whether thrones or dominions or principalities or authorities – all things were created through him and for him.' (Col. 1:16).

This quotation comes from the recently published *Catechism of the Catholic Church*, the first part of which expounds the creeds professed by Christians generally. The 'Apostles' Creed' was expanded at the Council of Nicea in the fourth century into the 'Nicene Creed'. Christian faith in an invisible 'angelic' world is expressed in the latter's opening clause: 'We believe in one God, the Father, the Almighty, maker of heaven and earth, of all that is, seen and unseen' (*visibilium et invisibilium*). The Catechism further quotes from the profession of faith of the Lateran Council of 1215 which affirms that God,

> from the beginning of time made at once (*simul*) out of nothing both orders of creatures, the spiritual and the corporeal, that is the angelic and the earthly, and then (*deinde*) the human creature, who as it were shares in both orders, being composed of spirit and body (Paragraph 327).

The Catechism goes on:

> The existence of the spiritual, non-corporeal beings that sacred Scripture usually calls 'angels' is a truth of faith. The witness of Scripture is as clear as the unanimity of Tradition (Paragraph 328).

Actually, the witness of Scripture is not so clear, except that angels are there witnessed to in a variety of ways, and Tradition is not unanimous in its understanding of the nature or function of angels, only that they are carried within it. The statement from the Fourth Lateran Council requires elucidation on all points: the 'time' of the angels' creation;

whether they are actually incorporeal; the ordering of angels and humans; and so on. Theologians have delved into these problems, sometimes clarifying them, sometimes creating further complications. Other disciplines have contributed to the discussion, such as metaphysics, cosmology, psychology and physics. I shall concentrate on 'the witness of Scripture', as the background of all Christian speculation on angels, and as a presentation of the angels of God in action, in relation to people.

Perhaps the strongest witness of the Bible to the nature of angels is that all their activity is *relational*, to God and the human race. In this they are congenial to our Christian understanding of God, and to living Christianity which is concerned with relationship. The Trinity is itself a relationship within the unity of the One God, revealed to us in the sending of the Son and the Holy Spirit, with whom we are each invited to personal relationship. The Church is a communion: every Christian is committed to mutual love, help and intercession, in relationships which are not broken by death. Within this web the angels operate, according to the Bible; its stories tell of angels helping and guiding, bringing revelations of God's relationship with his people. They never display a life of their own, and only rarely are they described as communicating with each other. They are either turned towards God in worship and praise, or towards the recipients of God's power, light and providence. They appear as essentially conjunctive, mediating between God and humankind.

Christ is the one true mediator (cf. 1 Tim. 2:5). In the simplest terms, his mediation is perfect, since he does not move between God and man, he *is* God and man. The mediating function of angels can be seen as made possible within the overall power of his mediation, manifested in the Incarnation. A mediator is one who is brought in between two parties to effect some kind of agreement or union between them. Christians believe that God created the human race to be united with him, and in order to bring this perfect union about he came himself to earth, uniting his divine nature with a human nature, Jesus Christ. The Incarnation was the focus, at one point in time, of the whole history of salvation, of bringing humanity to God. The processes of salvation history radiate from the life of Christ on earth, and include all the works of God throughout time. In the Bible we read about angels mediating between God and people; the stories explain how the ways of God can be perceived by us, then and now, and how through angels we may be helped to perceive the presence of divine power in the world. These angels, being in direct touch with God, bring in their very essence revelations of the will and operations of God. Their obedience can further divine providence to the benefit of all creation. Their action prepares us for, and is congruent with, our own direct perception of God's action, and thus for union with God.

Nevertheless, talking about 'spiritual power' does not entirely explain the appearances of angels as described in the Bible; there remains the question of the visible forms that angels take. It should not be taken for granted that in every narrated instance of angelic action they are actually described; there are incidents where no description of the angel is given. What is recounted is its effect on others and on events. Where it is described, the appearance of the angel is always in keeping with its particular function in the story or scene. The angel's mission from God is thus symbolically revealed to its recipient. When angels appear, when their invisible activity is made visible, then the form in which they appear may be perceived as a symbol of that activity. A symbol connects two entities. The word 'symbol' comes from the Greek verb *symbollein*: 'to bring together'. For instance, water can be a symbol of life; the common yet mysterious element, essential to daily life, stands for the deeper mystery of life itself. When, in the book of Genesis, Jacob sees the angels of God ascending and descending on a ladder set up between heaven and earth he is seeing the ever present reality of angelic activity symbolically represented; the angels are bringing together earth and heaven, they are seen as a connection between God and humankind. An explanation of the value of symbols serves to explain also the function of angels:

Symbols allow us to draw together different perceptions, different levels of understanding and meaning, different dimensions of human experience; symbols become the focal point at which the material and spiritual, the ordinary and the extraordinary, the human and the divine converge in human perception.[5]

The form taken by an angel is of importance because it reveals the angel's purpose. We cannot dismiss the form as simply a fanciful notion; it is part of the angel's message from God. But the problem of 'form' remains: while the shapes taken by angels may be symbolic, their existence as separate entities, appearing in various forms, demands explanation with regard to their actual life. Even though this is probably beyond human comprehension, there has always been speculation about it, and a great many theories have been put forward. Some of these will be discussed, but my emphasis throughout this book is on the activities of angels; we may learn something of what they are by looking at what they do, in the Bible text. In the novel *Mr Weston's Good Wine* by T. F. Powys, God, as Mr Weston, goes about on earth accompanied by Michael, a man. The author says, on the first appearance of Michael: 'We will note his behaviour; that is more important to us than the suddenness of his arrival, for it is from a man's behaviour when he does not know he is being watched that his character, as well as his situation and rank in the world, may be discovered.'[6]

The role of angels

This book is divided into four parts: angels are considered first as mediators, then as messengers, as ministers, and finally in relation to the end of time when comes the perfection of the kingdom of God. In the first part the mediatory nature of angels will be considered, along with corresponding functions. A parallel is drawn between angels and prophets; the link between the two is a recurring idea in the book. The prophet's ability to see angels brings him into conjunction with them, and his prophetic role is that of both mediator and messenger. Some theological, philosophical and ecclesiastical traditions enter the discussion, and the section closes with a chapter on the activities of evil spirits, headed by their traditional leader, Satan. It will be seen that the name Satan derives from a more equivocal spiritual intervention in the figure of 'the adversary'. This is necessarily the longest 'quarter' of the book, since here the foundations of further exploration are laid. It is followed by the section on the eponymous work of angels as messengers, which begins with the annunciation scenes in the Bible, and continues with other calls, given through angels, to Old Testament prophets and servants of God. Under the title 'ministers' comes the work of guardian angels, among other ministries, and here the angels' service to God in the form of constant praise and worship is considered. Traditionally the worship of the Church on earth is seen as a participation in the worship offered by the angels in heaven as described in the Bible. Again, we are in relation with the angels as we share in their praise and they share ours. The Dominican Cornelius Ernst has written: 'The only way in which we can understand, or see, an angel is precisely by being *with* an angel, by sharing a community with angels . . . We can share in a world of presences which, in Christian terms, can be concentrated at a particular privileged point, the presence which is the eucharistic liturgy.'[7] The final part, entitled 'Visions of the End', is concerned with apocalyptic vision, particularly as related in the Bible. The book closes with a chapter on Christ and his angels in the Gospels, with the climax of his resurrection and ascension where the angels play very important parts.

Angels in tradition, history and the Bible

Some explanation must be offered of my general approaches to tradition, history, and to the Bible text. First, the Bible: it will be noticed that the Old Testament stories are treated in the present tense, to convey the timeless quality of myth. The stories where angels figure give account of the nature of

18

belief in angels in the Judaeo-Christian heritage. As such, the historicity of the writings themselves is not relevant to the discussion. The Gospel stories, on the other hand, and the history of the early Church in the New Testament, are treated in the past tense. Their reality is historical as well as mythical; it is necessarily pinned to actual times and places while retaining its quality of myth.

An understanding of the word 'myth' is most important. Nowadays it can refer to a statement that is untrue or unreliable; that is not how I am using it. Myth is the explanation of things that cannot be explained in any other way except by a story. A true myth presents truth by means of the story. 'It is the significance of a myth that is its reality.'[8] Part of the power of the Old Testament stories is in their fascination simply as stories, and in their revelations of God's mysterious dealings with humankind, which continue through all time. They combine myth and revelation with the history of the Jewish people. (That history is a separate line of study which does not concern the subject of this book.) When angels appear in the stories it is usually at the point of deepest mystery, when the life of God touches most directly the lives of people. The New Testament is the story of the greatest mystery of all: when God came to live among us in Jesus Christ. The great events of the Gospels are things needing to be explained, and the story of the life of Christ is their explanation, continued in the ongoing story of his living presence in the Church. Again, in the Gospels and Acts angels appear when the pattern of God's providence is shown in a larger sense within the details of the narrative. It is like a spotlight coming on at key moments in a play, to reveal a hint of the denouement. Therefore studying these descriptions of angelic action takes us into the most dramatic scenes in both Old and New Testaments. If we are to understand the play, we should try to understand these highlighted moments, and what is their role in the drama.

Particular scenes in the Bible illustrate particular kinds of angelic action. Because the purpose of the book is to develop an understanding of angels, for the most part I do not cover the books of the Bible consecutively, but move forwards or backwards according to the subject under discussion, not according to chronology. I hope there will be no confusion as a result; I have tried to make the necessary transitions clear. Also, in discussing various traditions I do not follow the history of angelology in any methodical way. Inevitably historical developments of the Jewish tradition affect the imagery of their later writings; this is part of the Christian heritage, and is taken into account. However, I do not attempt any detailed examination of those developments that burgeoned during the immediately pre-Christian age, since their greater complexities have never found a way into Christian belief. Neither do I spend much time on the influence of Graeco-Roman mythology, which nevertheless did have a strong effect on Christian imagination, in particular on the iconography of angels. Where this effect is relevant to my discussion it is included, but the iconography has been set aside as a subject demanding its own scrutiny.

Rather than the history of angelic imagery, my interest has been in angels *within* history. In the Bible they intervene in the lives of individuals and groups. Sometimes they change the course of events. How far angels may be separated from time and matter are questions to be addressed; but however we define them, their connections with time and space must be different from ours. The paradox of atemporal beings involved in temporal circumstances echoes the paradox that is the being of God and all its works. God's messengers bring the eternal into time, and immortality into mortal perception. The more we learn about them, the more we may become aware of their presence, not only in stories, but here and now; in the liturgy, in personal life, and in creation. As spirits they may be apart from this world, but in action they are seen to be very much part of it. Their possible ministry in the physical universe will be considered, and the discussion frequently points out their involvement both symbolically and directly with the four elements: earth, air, fire and water. Angels meet people on the ground; they move through the air, and breathe out the word of God in their messages; they appear as fire and light; they reveal rivers of life, stand in the sea, and bring the sound of rushing waters. In all these ways they unite with creation to speak of the living creativity of God, present in everything God makes. In the Bible they speak about God, they also speak in his 'voice'. We should pay regard to them.

> . . . Redeem
> the time. Redeem
> the unread vision in the higher dream . . .
> the token of the word unheard, unspoken . . .
> (T. S. Eliot, *Ash Wednesday*)

Notes to Introduction

1. Cecil Collins, 'Hymn of Life', in *The Vision of the Fool* (Golgonooza Press, Ipswich, 1994).
2. See M. Boyce, *Zoroastrians* (Routledge, London, 1979); N. Forsyth, *The Old Enemy* (Princeton U.P., New Jersey, 1987); A. Cotterell, *A Dictionary of World Mythology* (O.U.P., Oxford, 1986).
3. E. E. Evans-Pritchard, *Nuer Religion* (O.U.P., Oxford, 1956).
4. All Biblical quotations are taken from the Revised Standard Version unless otherwise stated. Abbreviations used are JB for Jerusalem Bible and AV for Authorized Version (King James).
5. J. Baggley, *Doors of Perception* (London and Oxford, 1987) p. 33.
6. T. F. Powys, *Mr Weston's Good Wine* (Chatto and Windus, London, 1927) ch. 4.
7. Cornelius Ernst, OP, 'How to see an angel', in *Multiple Echo, Explorations in Theology*, ed. F. Kerr OP and T. Radcliffe OP (Darton, Longman and Todd, London, 1979) p. 200.
8. Cecil Collins, op.cit.

PART I

Mediators

*And he dreamed that there was a ladder set
up on earth, and the top of it reached
to heaven; and behold, the angels of God
were ascending and descending upon it.*
(Genesis 28:12)

1. Thresholds

All these things entered you
As if they were both
the door and what came through it.[1]
(SEAMUS HEANEY)

The Bible portrays angels in action. From time to time they enter the human world, revealing divine power, and when this happens events take a new turn: the appearance of angels has an effect. When they come into a scene a different light is shed on the narrative; for there is always a purpose in their entry, which ultimately is the purpose of God, furthered by the actions of angels. By their very presence, as much as by what they say and do, the angels have power to change people and events.

For instance, a story is told in the second book of Kings of how the prophet Elisha is able to defend the people of Israel, and himself, against the armies of Syria (2 Kgs 6:8–23). The king of Syria has repeatedly sent raiding parties into Israel, but every time they are forestalled by Israelite ambush. Calling his military advisers, he demands to see the betrayer: 'Will you not show me who of us is for the King of Israel?' (v. 11). It transpires that the informant is Elisha, the Israelite man of God, whose powers enable him to tell his king of discussions taking place even in the bedroom of the Syrian king, and so save the towns of Israel. Spies are despatched to locate Elisha. He is said to be in Dothan, a small town at the foot of the mountains north of Samaria. The king of Syria sends a division to capture Elisha; by night a heavily armed force of horse-drawn chariots (each with a driver and two or three bowmen) descends upon Dothan, ready to surround it at dawn. Elisha's manservant, Gehazi, going about his early-morning duties, suddenly sees the army in the distance. In terror he runs back to the prophet in the house.

> And the servant said, 'Alas, my master, what shall we do?' Elisha said, 'Fear not; for those who are with us are more than those who are with them.' Then Elisha prayed, and said, 'O Lord, I pray thee, open his eyes, that he may see.' So the Lord opened the eyes of the young man, and he saw, and behold, the mountain was full of horses and chariots of fire round about Elisha. (vv. 15–17)

Gehazi and his master stand looking up into the ring of hills during a silent moment before the noise of the Syrian army reaches them. The bare mountain is ablaze with what can only be the angelic host. It is manifested in likeness to the approaching enemy; chariots, symbols of martial strength. The chariots of God 'are thousands upon thousands' (Psalm 68:17). These chariots are not only more in number, but greater in power, higher in being, burning with divine fire. In the spectacle of the army of angels blazing on the mountain top, Gehazi is offered a sight of the source of his master's strength. As a prophet Elisha shares in divine power, which the angels represent. The fiery chariots and horses do not charge down from the mountains behind Dothan, but knowing himself surrounded by them Elisha faces the Syrians when they come, and again he prays: that as God had opened Gehazi's eyes to see the reality of the angels, so he might now close the eyes of the enemy to confuse them. The chariots of God are with Elisha, so he will reduce the Syrian chariots to chaos.

> And God struck them with blindness[2] in accordance with the prayer of Elisha. And Elisha said to them, 'This is not the way, neither is this the city; follow me, and I will bring you to the man whom you seek.' And he led them to Samaria (vv. 18–19).

There Elisha prays again: 'and the Lord opened their eyes,

and they saw, and lo, they were in the midst of Samaria.' The Syrians find themselves at the mercy of Israel, but Elisha will not allow his king to kill the captives: 'You shall not slay them' (v. 22). He must rather give them a good meal and send them back to their ruler. The Syrians are chastened by their experience, so the story ends: 'the Syrians came no more on raids into the land of Israel' (v. 23).

Elisha requests that Gehazi be allowed a share of his prophetic vision. As a prophet, a seer, Elisha possesses the gift of seeing what is really so. Gehazi is enabled to see the angels, who are already present; they do not arrive, they simply become visible to him. The prophet traverses the frontiers of the visible and invisible. He presents a sign of the possibility, for all of us, of seeing beyond the limitations of our immediate world, and participating in the fullness of reality. In this case, the angels complete the picture. Elisha knows they are there, as his defenders. The prophet stands on the boundary between his own world and that of the angels and sees both sides, without confusion and distortion. He knows clearly the majesty, the glory and the terror of the transcendent, because as a prophet he has something in common with the angels themselves. He presents an aura of holiness, which means that he is always viewed with respect, and some fear. The prophet knows that the power of the angels' majesty is nothing less than the power of God, ever present in creation. Paradoxically, the presence of God and the revelation of his angels are both awesome and reassuring. Reassurance comes with understanding, and with faith. It is the reassurance of divine power as salvation, not in a comfortable consolation, but with the knowledge that it can also be retribution. The reassurance of faith does not do away with fear, it transfigures fear into worship and love.

When Christ was surrounded by his enemies, come by night to arrest him, he said to his disciples, 'Do you think that I cannot appeal to my Father, and he will at once send me more than twelve legions of angels?' (Matt. 26:53). He was expecting the arrival of the soldiers, his disciples were not. They were afraid, so one of them drew his sword and attacked. Christ rebuked him (we recall Elisha's 'You shall not slay them') and reminded him of the invisible forces of God. ('Fear not,' said Elisha, 'for those who are with us are more than those who are with them.') Christ might have opened the eyes of his disciples to see the fiery legions, or struck the soldiers with blindness. Instead he went towards them, declaring himself to be the man they wanted. He was to redeem the world by the 'failure' of the cross, alone. His disciples did not see the angels and dispersed, in fear.

In 2 Kings the prophet Elisha receives his gift of prophetic vision from his master, Elijah, one of the greatest prophets of Israel. Elisha is the disciple of Elijah. At the time of Elijah's removal from this world (before the Dothan episode), when he stands at the threshold of death, Elisha asks to be given a double portion of his spirit (i.e. the inheritance of a firstborn, a double portion. cf. Deut. 21:17). 'You have asked a hard thing,' Elijah says; 'Yet, if you see me as I am being taken from you, it shall be so for you; but if you do not see me, it shall not be so' (2 Kgs 2:9–10). As they continue walking and talking together, 'a chariot of fire and horses of fire separated the two of them. And Elijah went up by a whirlwind into heaven. And Elisha saw it, and he cried, 'My father, my father!' (vv. 11–12). This chariot of fire also has an angelic function, prefiguring the army of chariots above Dothan, later in the book. The fiery chariot also denotes the close alliance between prophet and angel. But in the agony of parting Elisha can perceive only that the ascending flames and whirlwind are taking Elijah away; Elijah, who is himself called 'the chariots of Israel and its horsemen' (v. 12).[3] Who will be Israel's strength, if they are not to see the great prophet any more? It is only when the chariot disappears from sight, having become nothing but a single flame in the sky, that Elisha sees it for what it signifies: the prophetic power of Elijah. Elisha has seen into the world beyond, seen Elijah taken up with the chariot to become one with its fire. The sign gives him the assurance that he may now call Elijah 'my father'; he knows he will inherit Elijah's role, the chariot, with his endowment of the prophetic spirit.

Then Elisha notices Elijah's cloak lying on the ground where it had fallen from the prophet's shoulders when he was whirled up. This is the cloak that had been ritually thrown over Elisha when he was first called to follow Elijah (see 1 Kgs 19:19–21). Elisha remembers his master rolling the cloak and striking the river Jordan; the water divided to make a path for them to cross (2 Kgs 2:8). Elijah and Elisha had crossed over the river, to a new place beyond, from where Elijah was taken across another divide, into heaven. As though to test his dawning understanding, Elisha takes the mantle to the river again, and strikes the surface saying, 'Where is the Lord, the God of Elijah?' The waters part, and Elisha returns to the other side. The miracle is seen by a group of fellow prophets who are waiting for him there. They bow to him, saying, 'The spirit of Elijah rests on Elisha' (vv. 13–15). In his turn Elisha, on his deathbed, will be addressed by King Joash as 'My father, the chariots of Israel' (2 Kgs 13:14).

When Elijah casts his mantle over Elisha to make him a disciple he is performing a human ritual that will be ratified by divine action at the appearance of the fiery chariot. The two miraculous partings of the river Jordan recounted in 2 Kings re-enact the original crossing of Jordan by the Israelites, long before, with Joshua at their head, as told in the book of Joshua. Joshua's call to succeed Moses as leader is also marked by human and divine action. At God's command Moses designates Joshua his successor and lays his hands on him (see Deut. 31:3f. and 34:9). Later, after a miraculous crossing of the river Jordan, Joshua is preparing to take the city of Jericho, when an angel appears to him. The Israelites are camped at Gilgal, a place Joshua has made sacred by setting up twelve stones taken from the bed of the Jordan, to mark the miracle of the twelve tribes walking across dry-shod (Josh. ch. 4).

When Joshua was near Jericho, he raised his eyes and saw a man standing there before him, grasping a naked sword. Joshua walked towards him and said to him, 'Are you with us or with our enemies?' He answered, 'No, I am captain of the army of Yahweh and now I come.' Joshua fell on his face to the ground and worshipped him and said, 'What are my Lord's commands to his servant?' The captain of the army of Yahweh answered Joshua, 'Take your sandals off your feet, for the place you are standing on is holy.' And Joshua obeyed. (Josh. 5:13–15. JB)

This brief episode confirms that Joshua has received a 'portion' of the spirit of Moses. His sight is enlarged to see the angelic commander, and he hears the same injunction that Moses heard, to reverence the very ground on which he stands, since he is in the presence of God as represented by the angel. He participates in Moses' call to lead the Israelites to the promised land.

Seeing and not seeing

In all these stories emphasis is laid on seeing. I have recounted them in order to make two points initially: the first is that the Bible shows that angels are a constant presence in the world. They provide active power and support, mediating the power and support of God. They become visible, in the stories, so that certain people may benefit from the recognition of their presence, signifying the presence of God. The second point, however, is that a special kind of 'seeing' is required before angels become visible. In these stories, seeing angels manifested in appropriate forms is proof of the gift or inheritance of prophetic vision. The disciple has been dependent on his master for the gift of sight. It is, however, a free gift from God which may be given to anyone at any time. In addition, the place where the vision is granted takes on a special significance.

When Joshua 'lifted up his eyes and looked' he had recently crossed the river Jordan, arriving on new ground. The angel tells him it is holy ground, which Joshua has already recognized, and marked by the setting up of twelve stones. Very often, in the Bible, when a vision of angels is granted the seer moves on to new ground, like Elijah and Elisha also crossing the river Jordan. The earth upon which the vision takes place, where the angel figure is made visible, becomes a threshold of heaven. For, though the angels have been shown to be constantly present on earth, they mediate the light of heaven, and seeing them is to see into heaven, from earth. A threshold is a crossing point; it is neither one place nor another, but lies in between. To move on to new ground may be dangerous; a great risk is taken, as when Joshua approaches the enemy city of Jericho. He has been taken across the Jordan, into hostile territory, and when the angel appears Joshua is on the very threshold of Jericho, which in the event will be given into his hands by a miracle.

In the book of Genesis we read how Jacob, the ancestor of Joshua and his people, sets out on a journey into entirely strange country. He is escaping from his brother whom he has tricked:

> Jacob left Beersheba, and went toward Haran. And he came to a certain place, and stayed there that night, because the sun had set. Taking one of the stones of the place, he put it under his head and lay down in that place to sleep. And he dreamed that there was a ladder set up on the earth, and the top of it reached to heaven; and behold, the angels of God were ascending and descending on it (Gen. 28:10–12).

Jacob has lain down to sleep in 'a certain place', somewhere along his journey between Beersheba and Haran. In his sleep Jacob's eyes are opened to see the place as a crossing point. He is at the foot of a stairway rising from earth to heaven, upon which the angels of God move continually up and down, traversing the space between.

> And behold, the Lord stood above it and said, 'I am the Lord, the God of Abraham your father and the God of Isaac; the land on which you lie I will give to you and to your descendants' (v. 13).

Jacob hears the promise which had been made to his grand-father, Abraham, and his father Isaac.

> Then Jacob awoke from his sleep and said, 'Surely the Lord is in this place; and I did not know it.' And he was afraid, and said, 'How awesome is this place! This is none other than the house of God, and this is the gate of heaven' (vv. 16–17).

Having arrived at the place, Jacob finds himself on holy ground. He describes it as the dwelling-place of God. His fear is engendered by the experience of God's proximity. The text does not say that Jacob sees God, but that God is somehow present, and his words are heard. God himself has no voice, no visible shape, no 'face'. 'You cannot see my face,' God would tell Moses, making explicit the danger of encounter with the Divine, 'for man shall not see me and live' (Exod. 33:20). What Jacob sees is a stairway with angels going up and down it. From above come the words of God. The gulf between heaven and earth is bridged, by the angels, and Jacob knows that the place where he lies is now close to God. He calls it the 'gate of heaven'.

A gateway is a threshold, neither outside nor inside a town or settlement; it is the place of passage and con-course, where traffic moves to and fro, meetings occur, and ceremonial processions pass through. It is the only means of lawful entry. Jacob sees the angels of God ascending and descending, a continuous activity, rather like a pathway of ants on the side of a hollow tree, appearing as ceaseless movement, entirely dedicated to its purpose.[4] They are constantly crossing over the divide between God and humankind. That their action should be described as 'ascending and descending' accords with the universal re-ligious concept of the divine as 'above': the mysterious home of God is imagined to be beyond the mystery of the sky. Human efforts to reach up to God are exampled in sacred towers and temples – the ziggurats of Mesopotamia, the holy city of Jerusalem built on a mountain, cathedral spires, all ritual pilgrimages of ascent. Jacob's vision reveals to him that the angels of God unite 'the Most High' with people on earth. God comes 'down' to them. Jacob is given a promise by God: 'Behold, I am with you and will keep you wherever you go' (Gen. 28:15). Jacob's feeling of awe in the presence of God is accompanied by a great reassurance. Like Gehazi, his eyes are opened to see that God is actively assisting him. The angels' mediation touches his deepest uncertainty; he left home to escape his brother's vengeance, and is setting out into the unknown. Now he can continue his journey with confidence.

In John's Gospel a connection is made between the vision of Jacob (who is later called 'Israel') and the final glory of Christ: when Jesus met Nathanael, and called him 'an Israelite indeed', Nathanael expressed amazement at his prophetic vision, and called him 'Son of God, King of Israel'. Jesus replied, 'Because I said to you, I saw you under the fig tree, do you believe? You shall see greater things than these. Truly, truly, I say to you, you will see heaven opened, and the angels of God ascending and descending upon the Son of Man.' (John 1:47–51). Once again the emphasis is on seeing. Jesus opens Nathanael's eyes to a far wider vision than a mere trick of sight. His reference to Jacob relates himself and his disciples to that moment of the descent of God to earth, and to the promise made to Jacob. He is identified with Jacob, a son of man upon whom the angels descend and ascend. Contained in the allusion is the identification of Christ as mediator, the ascent and descent of the angels representing his coming to earth bringing the voice of God. He can be seen as prophet and angel, and is frequently referred to as more than both.

Signs of contradiction

Further on in John's Gospel Jesus is reported as saying, 'I am the door of the sheep[fold]' (10:7). He himself is the gateway, the threshold, the crossing point. Jesus goes on to say, 'I am the good shepherd' (v. 11), apparently a contradictory statement; how can he be both the door and the shepherd who goes through the door to call his sheep? The answer must be because he is both God and man; he was, in Luke's phrase, born to be a 'sign of contradiction' (Luke 2:34, my translation of the Greek *antilegomenon*). It is so for the angels too; whenever they appear in this world, angels signal the existence of a greater one. The chariots defending Elisha are apparently on fire, but it is not earthly fire, which would simply burn them up. They are made of fire, as are the chariot and horses that drive between Elisha and Elijah, separating Elijah from this world, to be taken into heaven. The angel who speaks to Moses on Mount Horeb appears as a flame of fire from the middle of a bush, but the bush is not burning. Again we see there is a 'sign of contradiction'. Angels are figures of their very function, which is to cross over, to move between earth and heaven. They are both the door and what comes through it.

In the texts that describe them, angels very often take on forms that bring together the disparate. The most usual image of them is in fact monstrous: men with wings, and as such it is a fitting image, since monsters also symbolize a transition from one category to another. They do not belong to any one sort, but are composed of incongruous elements, and images of mixed creatures commonly represent other spirit worlds; for examples: satyrs, unicorns, mermaids, the Egyptian dog-headed god, Anubis. Because they do not conform to the natural limitations of one species they denote supernatural power. Throughout the ancient east there are figures which appear as guardians of the doors of temples and palaces; magnificent beasts with bodies of lions or bulls, birds' claws, wings rising from their shoulders, and human heads or faces. Considered as 'threshold' creatures they mark the difference between outside and inside, between here and there. They are visible reminders of the need to recognize that there is a threshold, a place of transition, and that different worlds lie on either side. They are therefore suited to defend the doorway of a sacred building. They also appear as supporters of the king's throne. Again the purpose is dual;

to defend the royal person and to emphasize the spiritual significance of the seat of sovereign authority, for the king ruled by divine power.

Angels may also stand as guardians of doors and gates. In his Apocalypse John writes of his vision of the new, heavenly Jerusalem. An angel carried him away in the spirit, he says, 'to a great high mountain, and showed me the holy city, Jerusalem coming down out of heaven from God . . . It had a great, high wall with twelve gates, and at the gates twelve angels, and on the gates the names of the twelve tribes of the sons of Israel were inscribed.' (Rev. 21:10–12). In Dante's *Purgatorio* there is an angel at the gate of Purgatory, and angels at each level permitting the next ascent.

In the book of Genesis, when God sends Adam from the garden of Eden, he establishes 'the cherubim' to the east of the garden, 'and a flaming sword which turned every way, to guard the way to the tree of life' (Gen. 3:24). The Hebrew word *kerub*, plural form *kerubim*, may be derived from *kiribu*, the Assyrian name of a winged bull, guardian of doorways, but the theory is not verified.[5] However, in other parts of the Bible the name is applied to winged creatures of hybrid character with tutelary function, so Genesis could be describing how God establishes some such pair of spiritual guardians at the eastern entrance to Eden. If we do imagine these four-footed doorkeeping creatures there, the turning fiery sword must stand on its own, for they would not be sword-bearers. The Hebrew description of the sword indicates a continuous revolving movement. Winged god-like monsters, flanking a revolving sword of fire, present a formidable barrier. They are preventing access to the tree of life which symbolizes the very life of God and his inaccessible glory.

When the wandering Israelites construct a tabernacle, or elaborate tent, for the worship of God, under divine instruction they make figures of 'cherubim' to represent a guard over the innermost sanctuary. The cherubim take on the double significance of guardians of the holy place, and supports for the 'mercy seat', the *kapporeth*, which is the golden top of the ark of the covenant. It is the point to which God would descend, in his concern for his people, each time the tent is re-erected (Exod. 25:18–22). In this psalm they are pleading with God to give them help:

> Give ear, O Shepherd of Israel,
> thou who leadest Joseph like a flock!
> Thou who art enthroned upon the cherubim, shine
> forth before Ephraim and Benjamin and Manasseh;
> Stir up thy might, and come to save us!
>
> (Psalm 80:1–2)

The cherubim of Genesis and Exodus have come to be considered as angel figures, part of God's spirit creation of threshold beings. The cry of the Jews in the psalm voices the human predicament: Jacob saw heaven opened, the angels of God uniting it with earth, and he heard God's promise to be with him and his descendants, yet the way to God was sometimes barred by angels, and his glory hidden by their protecting wings, in the sacred place which only the high priest could enter. Christ told Nathanael that the true vision of heaven would come, that he would see heaven opened. The veil of the temple was finally torn, and the Son of God who is also the Son of Man entered the sanctuary. 'When Christ appeared as a high priest of the good things that have come, then through the greater and more perfect tent (not made with hands, that is, not of this creation) he entered once for all into the Holy Place, taking not the blood of goats and calves but his own blood, thus securing an eternal redemption' (Heb. 9:11–12).

Those whose eyes are opened can realize that the static guarding creatures are done away with for all time in the passion and resurrection of Christ. The doorway to heaven is open, and there is perpetual movement over the threshold. This is what Jacob saw in his vision: the eternal reality of that open door. The vision is outside time, redemption is secured for past, present and future. Christians may believe that the angels' purpose is to lead us to heaven through Christ, the door, helping us to 'go in and out and find pasture' (John 10:9). Angels once barred the way, so it is fitting, says Meister Eckhart, the fourteenth-century German preacher, that 'with the angels and through the angels and by the divine light the soul must strive to return to God.'[6]

Notes for Part I Chapter 1

[1] Seamus Heaney, from 'Markings', in *Seeing Things* (Faber and Faber, London, 1991) p. 9.

[2] The Hebrew word for 'blindness' is *sanwerim* which occurs in only one other place in the Bible: Genesis 19:11, where the inhabitants of Sodom are struck with blindness, by the action of angels. (See Part III, ch. 1.) It has been suggested that *sanwerim* could have implied blinding light, such as Paul's experience on the road to Damascus. It certainly implies sudden strokes, perhaps blinding flashes emanating from the angels (cf. E. A. Speiser, *Genesis*, in Anchor Bible Series, New York 1964). Speiser suggests that *sanwerim* is based on the Akkadian *sunwurum*, 'having extraordinary brightness'. Brown-Driver-Briggs Hebrew Lexicon admits no positive derivations.

[3] 'Chariotry', or 'chariot'; the Hebrew word *rechev* is in the singular, used as a collective noun. As Israel's 'chariotry' the two great prophets were, each in his turn, the strength and the sign of nobility of the Israelite nation (cf. 1 Kings 1.5 and 10.26). In the singular, the prophet as the 'chariot of Israel and its horsemen' could signify the special chariot of the king, where he stood as a figurehead. In warfare it was a sign of direction and encouragement, and the seat of counsel (cf. 1 Kings 20.33 and 22.32, 35).

[4] John of Damascus (eighth century) describes the angels as 'ever in motion', *aeikinetos*. See *The Orthodox Faith* II, 3 (Patrologia Graeca 94, col. 865; Paris, 1857–66).

[5] Brown-Driver-Briggs, Hebrew Lexicon (Hendrikson, Peabody, Mass., 1979).

6 M. Walshe ed., *Meister Eckhart*, Vol. II (Element Books, Shaftsbury, 1981) p. 12.

2. Encounters on Holy Ground

In the streets of the still town
I met a man in the lamplight,
He stood in the alley that led down
To the harbour and the sea out of sight.

'What do you want?' he asked me,
'Who are you looking for in this place?'
The houses echoed us emptily
And the lamp shone on his face.[1]

(PETER LEVI)

In the stories we have been discussing, the movement of angelic creatures is described in spatial images: they come *down* and go *up*; they *encircle*; they travel *between* people; go *through* doorways, pass *in* and *out*. Yet angels, as spirits, are defined as existing without the same confines of space and time that we experience. So, in taking action on earth they are seen to unite a non-spatial, non-temporal world with this one. We underestimate their effectiveness if we read their appearances as simply a momentary stepping into our time, leaving it again when they leave the story. The words used in the narratives should not restrict the angels' activity, in our minds, but be taken as a necessity of language. Nevertheless angels do appear *in* the world, and when this happens their presence reveals the presence of their world as integral to ours. They invite those who see them to step over the boundaries and limitations of the material universe and to recognize its share in the boundless and unlimited, so that new possibilities open up before them. In the Bible these encounters take place at particular locations, and where the unity of heaven and earth is revealed that place is sanctified;

it becomes 'holy ground'. The stories signify that earth can be the visible sign of heaven. Creation has the capacity to show forth the greater reality from which it springs, and in which it shares. This greater reality is the source of life, sanctifying all that exists, but to focus our understanding we need specific demonstrations. The fact that the Son of God walked on our terrain sanctifies the whole earth, but the particular country where Jesus lived is called 'the Holy Land'. It was there that he 'went in and out among us' (Acts 1:21). Scenes where angels enter space and time can present a visible sign of their constant and universal presence.

Often the vision of angels occurs, as we have noted, when someone is taken to new ground. It might be a place with some significance already, or be unnamed, but afterwards it remains sacred by right of its legend. Holiness is written into it. By ritual it may be marked out for commemoration. The sacred place is more than just a reminder, however; it *is* holy, opened up to the primal reality of heaven. Here is a threshold; 'this is the gate of heaven', says Jacob, 'this is the house of God.' Jacob takes the stone he used for a pillow, stands it on end, and consecrates it with oil. He gives the place a new name: Bethel, 'house of God'. The stone itself shared in the vision, while his head rested on it as he slept. Jacob's ceremony confers upon it the full significance of his dream. He returns to Bethel later, and receives there a further seal of blessing from God.

The book of Chronicles tells how the temple of Jerusalem was built upon the site of a threshing floor, where King David saw the angel of God standing. The text is an elaboration of the second book of Samuel, chapter 24. David confesses that he has sinned in taking a census of the people, and as a requital God sends a plague; 'the angel of the Lord destroying throughout all the territory of Israel' (1 Chr. 21:12) God halts the plague just before it reaches Jerusalem.

The Lord said to the destroying angel, 'It is enough; now stay your hand.' And the angel of the Lord was standing by the threshing floor of Ornan the Jebusite. And David lifted up his eyes and saw the angel of the Lord standing between earth and heaven, and in his hand a drawn sword stretched over Jerusalem. (1 Chr. 21:15–16)

After his prayer for reconciliation, David buys the threshing floor.

Then David said, 'Here shall be the house of the Lord God and here the altar of burnt offering for Israel.' (22:1)

The threshing floor is where the angel stood and God gave forgiveness. David first consecrates it as an altar; later his son Solomon would build the temple there (see 2 Chr. 3:1) and it became the most sacred place of Jewish worship. Jesus was enraged when he saw its holy precincts abused; speaking for himself as God, he rebuked the abusers: 'My house shall be called a house of prayer; but you make it a den of robbers' (Matt. 21:13). This is the home of God, this is the gate of heaven.

David, like Jacob, would have placed a stone on the holy place, for the altar. The threshing floor itself would have been a circular stone structure with a raised edge to contain the grain as it was threshed. The raised edge is, of course, the threshold. (Our word describes the high sill built across the doorways at either end of a straight passage where the threshing was done in old farmhouses.) At Gilgal Joshua had the twelve stones laid in a circle; the name Gilgal means 'circle' or 'wheel'. It became a holy place which figures several times in the Old Testament.[2]

Holy places, specified by story, name, buildings, sacred purposes, etc. are signs of heaven reminding us that earth is not our home. 'Here we have no lasting city, but we seek the city which is to come' (Heb. 13:14). We are travellers, pilgrims. Jacob, travelling to Haran, saw angels on the way, and again on the way back twenty years later. We shall return to Jacob after discussing two or three other appearances of angels to people who are on a journey. In these scenes the angels do more than simply manifest their presence, they act upon the people in question, changing them, or pointing them in a different direction, interrupting their journey, sometimes with violence. These angels exercise their mediation by bringing about a new movement. What has gone before is halted. What is to come may clarify the past, and will be an entirely new future. In an interval of time and upon a transitional piece of ground the angel effects the beginning of another phase of action, which will further the purpose of God.

Hagar and the angel of God

The first appearance in the Bible of an angel named as such is to Hagar, the Egyptian maidservant of Sarai, Abram's wife. Hagar has conceived a child by Abram with Sarai's permission, but flees from Sarai's resentment and jealousy.

> The angel of the Lord found her by a spring of water in the wilderness, the spring on the way to Shur. And he said, 'Hagar, maid of Sarai, where have you come from and where are you going?' (Gen. 16:7–8)

The angel comes to Hagar at a 'crossing point': the oasis is the pausing place for people and animals, it is 'on the way' to Shur, neither here nor there. The angel's question highlights the nature of the place and the nature of Hagar's journey which is aimless.

There are several remarkable things about this first angelic visitation recorded in Hebrew scripture. Hagar is a woman, an Egyptian, and a slave, all inferior categories. Her son Ishmael is destined to live and die in opposition to the chosen people of God. (The Hebrew term in v. 12b and ch. 25, v. 18b is: 'in the face of his brothers' which in each context evidently means 'against them' rather than 'in their presence'. The Ishmaelites are traditionally seen as the founders of the Arab tribes who will tragically oppose the tribes of Israel; ch. 25, vv. 12–18.) But Hagar's desolation and fear are seen by God, and his angel is sent to give strength and direction to the outcast, and to inform her of her role. For the reader, the scene may prefigure the contrariness of Ishmael's destiny ('his hand against every man, and every man's hand against him', v. 12) by presenting a contrast with other, later, angelic interruptions. Here the angel turns Hagar back the way she has come, rather than forwarding her on her journey. We are told the angel 'found' her, as though it had come behind her instead of confronting her. Hagar herself gives a name to the divine being who speaks to her; she calls it 'God who sees me' (my translation of the Hebrew *el roi*), emphasizing the fact that God has seen her even as she tried to escape, perhaps from God. She expresses wonder that she can still see, is still alive (v. 13).

Hagar is told to call her child Ishmael, which means 'God hears'. The name receives its warrant later when Hagar once again flees from Sarah's[3] jealousy, this time with her growing son. They are dying of thirst in the wilderness and God hears the boy's crying.

> And the angel of God called to Hagar from heaven... 'Arise, lift up the lad, and hold him fast with your hand; for I will make him a great nation.' Then God opened her eyes, and she saw a well of water. (Gen. 21:17–19)

The intervention of the angel on Hagar's journeys reveals the all-seeing and purposeful compassion of God. Here the seeing and hearing are done by God. Only at the end are we told that Hagar's eyes are 'opened' to see the saving water, though she has been clear-sighted towards God all along. She represents the despised and rejected whom God never forgets, and also the humble who never forget God.

The story of Balaam

Balaam, a famous soothsayer, needed to be turned towards God by an angel who barred his way. His story, in the book of Numbers, takes place at the time of Moses, towards the end of the Israelites' wanderings in the deserts east of the Dead Sea. They are camped in the plains of Moab, and have ruthlessly overcome many of the local tribes. Balak, a king of the Moabites, views their encampment on the borders of his territory with trepidation. He and the elders of Midian decide to pay for a curse to be pronounced on the Israelites. They send messengers to fetch Balaam the diviner, who lives a long way further east, near the Euphrates river. Balaam pays allegiance to God, the God of Israel, and God says to Balaam, 'You shall not go with them; you shall not curse the people, for they are blessed.' (Num. 22:12)

Balaam sends the messengers back to Balak, who will not accept the refusal, but commissions higher emissaries carrying greater rewards for Balaam. This time God tells him he may go, provided he does only what God commands him. In the morning Balaam sets off eagerly with the Moabite princes. 'But God's anger was kindled because he went; and the angel of the Lord took his stand in the way as his adversary' (v. 22). Evidently Balaam's intention is misdirected. He is setting out blindly, on a wrong path. Balaam rides along on his ass,

> and the ass saw the angel of the Lord standing in the road, with a drawn sword in his hand; and the ass turned aside out of the road, and went into the field; and Balaam struck the ass, to turn her into the road. Then the angel of the Lord stood in a narrow path between the vineyards, with a wall on either side. And when the ass saw the angel of the Lord, she pushed against the wall, and pressed Balaam's foot against the wall; so he struck her again. Then the angel of the Lord went ahead and stood in a narrow place, where there was no way to turn either to the right or to the left. When the ass saw the angel of the Lord, she lay down under Balaam; and Balaam's anger was kindled, and he struck the ass with his staff. Then the Lord opened the mouth of the ass, and she said to Balaam, 'What have I done to you, that you struck me these three times?' (vv. 23–8)

Balaam then threatens the ass, but she remonstrates with him again. 'Then the Lord opened the eyes of Balaam, and he saw the angel of the Lord standing in the way, with his drawn sword in his hand; and he bowed his head, and fell on his face.' (v. 31) 'Behold, I have come forth to withstand you, because your way is perverse before me,' says the angel. Balaam confesses his fault and offers to return home, but the angel says, 'Go with the men; but only the word which I bid you, that shall you speak.' (vv. 32 and 35)

Sight and speech are the key motifs in this story. As soon as the ass speaks, another world is entered, one where all possibilities are open, where language is granted to every creature. It is like the world inhabited by La Fontaine, seventeenth-century poet and fabulist, who wrote: *'Le loup, en langue des dieux, parle au chien, dans mes ouvrages.'* (In my works the wolf speaks to the dog in the tongue of the gods.) The only other place in the Bible where an animal speaks is in the garden of Eden. Balaam steps into this other world unconsciously, without even a tremble of the focus, so blind is he still. He is simply angry with the ass. As soon as he sees the angel, Balaam prostrates himself before it. At that moment of humiliation Balaam sheds his previous existence and takes on a new one; he loses the impotent language of divination, and is given a new language, the word of God (albeit only for a time). When he first meets Balak, Balaam says to him, 'Lo, I have come to you! Have I now any power at all to speak anything? The word that God puts in my mouth, that must I speak.' (v. 38)

Balak takes Balaam up into the hills where they can see the Israelite camp. Three times Balak leads him to higher vantage points. The view of the camp becomes wider and wider, just as the angel led him, three times, into a narrower place. God extends Balaam's vision from the blind alley of wrong conceptions, to a breadth whereby he appreciates the glory of the people of God spread out in space and time before him.

And Balaam lifted up his eyes, and saw Israel encamping tribe by tribe. And the spirit of God came upon him and he took up his discourse and said, 'The oracle of Balaam son of Beor, the oracle of the man whose eye is opened . . . How fair are your tents, O Jacob, your encampments, O Israel! . . . Blessed be every one who blesses you, and cursed be every one who curses you.' (24:2–3, 5 and 9)

With the increasing width of vision, Balaam's poetic discourse develops, until his final prophecy reaches heights of lyricism and foresight:

> I see him, but not now;
> I behold him, but not nigh.
> A star shall come forth out of Jacob,
> and a sceptre shall rise out of Israel . . .
>
> (24:17)

At the moment of vision Balaam becomes a true prophet, in the manner of Elisha. For what Balaam sees, when he looks down on the tents of Israel, is what is already true: God has blessed the tribes of Jacob with his covenant to Abraham, and in them all his people, which means the whole human race, redeemed in Christ the 'star' and the 'sceptre'. Balaam is not called to bless them, but to pronounce the existing grace of God's promise.

An angel may intercept a journey

In the book of Genesis a figure appears in the story of Joseph, who points Joseph towards his destiny. Joseph has been sent off by his father, Jacob, to bring news of his brothers who are pasturing sheep away from home. Joseph sets out, alone,

and a man found him wandering in the fields; and the man asked him, 'What are you seeking?' 'I am seeking my brothers,' he said, 'tell me, I pray you, where they are pasturing the flock.' And the man said, 'They have gone away, for I heard them say, Let us go to Dothan.' So Joseph went after his brothers, and found them at Dothan. (Gen. 37:15–17)

Such a slight incident may be passed over without notice in the dramatic story of Joseph, but, once again, this scene is a turning point. If Joseph did not find his brothers, and simply returned home, he would not arrive in Egypt, for it is when he approaches them at Dothan that the brothers decide first to kill him, then to leave him at the bottom of the well. Joseph's fate eventually involves the whole family of Israel, and leads to the miraculous exodus from Egypt several generations later. The 'man' is, therefore, a highly significant figure. He stands at a possible division of the ways for Joseph, and directs him on God's way. The scene carries signs of an angelic encounter; this modern poem might be describing it:

Everything flows. Even a solid man,
A pillar to himself and to his trade,
All yellow boots and stick and soft felt hat,

Can sprout wings at the ankle and grow fleet
As the god of fair days, stone posts, roads and crossroads,
Guardian of travellers and psychopomp.[4]

Ambiguous figures such as this appear in many different scenes in the Bible, and another strange incident on a journey is related in the book of Exodus, where Moses experiences a divine confrontation while on his way to Egypt. He has been living in Midian, where he married Zipporah, a daughter of Jethro, 'the priest of Midian'. Zipporah bore Moses a son. While Moses was tending Jethro's sheep on Mount Horeb God spoke to him through the angel of fire in the bush, and instructed him to return to Egypt. He is to lead the Israelites out of slavery. Taking his wife and son with him, Moses sets off on the long journey to Egypt.

47

At a lodging place on the way the Lord met him and sought to kill him. Then Zipporah took a flint and cut off her son's foreskin and touched Moses' feet with it, and said, 'Surely you are a bridegroom of blood to me!' So he let him alone. Then it was that she said, 'You are a bridegroom of blood,' because of the circumcision. (Exod. 4:24–6)

This mysterious passage has no straightforward interpretation, and the Hebrew is unclear, but it seems to say that somewhere on the road between Midian and Egypt God sends an assailant to Moses because he had failed to fulfil the command of circumcision. The divine spirit (the Septuagint, the Greek version of the Hebrew Old Testament, translates: *angelos kyriou*, 'angel of the Lord') who challenges him on the way is set to overcome him, until Zipporah performs the rite of circumcision on their son, and then marks Moses with the boy's blood. The real point of the story must be that Moses had not been circumcised. Zipporah's action is a symbolic circumcision of her husband. The Hebrew Bible often employs the word for 'feet' as a euphemism for the genitals. The blood is a sacramental sign.

The three verses of text interrupt not only the journey, but the whole story of Moses. In this vivid scene a crucial action takes place. If Moses was uncircumcised his position as Israel's lawgiver is untenable. Other questions also are posed by the account of his early years. Almost from birth he is estranged from his own people. His upbringing, in the house of Pharaoh, removes him from Hebrew society and custom. When he tries to act in their defence, one of the Hebrews challenges him, and Moses is forced to escape to Midian, a foreign land (Exod. 2:11–15). Now he is returning to Egypt at God's command to lead his people out, a people to whom he is a stranger. Unless Moses bears the mark of circumcision, the sign of God's covenant with Israel, he cannot ratify that covenant for all generations to come. There has to be a central myth to explain these mysteries surrounding Moses.

The attacking angel appears at night in a lodging place on the way. Time and place are in keeping with the mystery. As soon as Zipporah performs the ritual circumcision of both father and son, the spirit releases Moses. 'So he let him alone.' The phrase suggests that the agent of God has been actually grappling with Moses, with intent to kill him. Zipporah averts his wrath by her actions and words. She first circumcises her son. He is called Gershom, which means 'a stranger here'. The circumcision now marks him as belonging to God's holy people, no longer a foreigner. Moses also had the stamp of a foreigner until the vital act is performed, through the blood of his only son. Now he is no longer separated from God, or from the people of God, his own kin. There are allusions in the story to the coming passover, and from that to the Christian paschal mystery. At the passover the destroying angel is averted from the Hebrew households by the mark of blood on the doorposts (Exod. 12:13). A further connection is signalled by the fact that the passover angel is commanded to kill all the firstborn sons of Egypt; God had told Moses before he set out on his journey to Egypt that this would happen. Moses is saved, as he had also been at his birth, by the courage and insight of a woman. In this incident at the inn the woman is caught up, with Moses, in the power of the angel of God. The action of the angel brings about the all-important change in Moses; he is marked out for his destiny.

Jacob wrestles with an angel

Angels come to meet people face to face on the road, sometimes with violence and the sword, and after the confrontation a change is effected. Jacob's vision of the angelic stairway to heaven came to him as he set out alone for the north. He would not return until twenty years later. On his long journey back, he, like Moses, is attacked by a mysterious assailant. Shortly before, he is met on the road by a whole army of angels.

From the beginning of the story of Jacob, he and his twin

brother Esau are set in opposition to each other, even before they are born:

> And Isaac prayed to the Lord for his wife, because she was barren; and the Lord granted his prayer, and Rebekah his wife conceived. The children struggled together [Hebrew, lit., 'struck or thrust against'] within her; and she said, 'If it is thus, why do I live?' So she went to enquire of the Lord. And the Lord said to her, 'Two nations are in your womb, and two peoples, born of you, shall be divided; the one shall be stronger than the other, the elder shall serve the younger.' (Gen. 25:21–3)

Esau is born first, and after him Jacob, grasping his brother's heel (vv. 25–6). Esau is always stronger, Jacob in fear of him. Esau sells his birthright to Jacob, for food. By deception Jacob obtains the firstborn's blessing from Isaac. After this he flees from Esau's threat to kill him. Even after the space of twenty years, and the promise from God in the vision of angels, Jacob is still afraid of Esau as he returns home with all the rewards of his labours and guile.

Pursued by Laban, his equally shrewd father-in-law and uncle, Jacob's caravan has reached Gilead, south of the Jabbok river. There Laban catches up with him. They make a truce, and Laban returns home. Jacob is at last free of servitude. He is alone, at the head of his own family company.

> Jacob went on his way, and the angels of God met him; and when Jacob saw them he said, 'This is God's army!' So he called the name of the place Mahanaim [or 'Two Camps']. (32:1–2)

No hint is given in the narrative as to the meaning of this encounter on the road. The story is told from Jacob's viewpoint, and he seems to see the army of God as an affirmation of his own prosperity: Jacob's camp is matched by the camp of the angelic host. In the next verse we are told that Jacob sends messengers ahead of him to his brother. Jacob is now in a position to inform Esau of all his successes. But when the messengers return with the news that Esau is on his way with four hundred men, Jacob's fear returns. The glory of 'Two camps' dwindles. He would have nothing without God's gift, and he needs the help of God to save it. He divides his train in two, to save at least half from Esau, and he prays:

> 'I am not worthy of the least of all the steadfast love and all the faithfulness which thou hast shown to thy servant, for with only my staff I crossed this Jordan; and now I have become two companies.' (v. 10)

The silent appearance of the angels has turned Jacob to God once more. God does not forget his promises, yet the lifelong struggle with Esau continues.

> 'Deliver me, I pray thee, from the hand of my brother, for I fear him, lest he come and slay us all, the mothers with the children.' (v. 11)

Esau's lands lie further to the south. Jacob's aim is to move westwards, across the river Jordan into the promised land of Canaan where, in the southern part, lies his father's home. He is travelling in borderland country, crossed by the river Jabbok, an eastern tributary of the Jordan. At this point Jacob is camped by the ford of the Jabbok, a watering and crossing place. He sends all his flocks and herdsmen, in spaced groups, southwards towards Esau. He and his family lodge that night in the camp on the northern bank.

> And in the same night he arose and took his two wives, his two maids, and his eleven children, and crossed the ford of the Jabbok. He took them and sent them across the stream, and likewise everything that he had. And Jacob was left alone. (vv. 22–4)

Now Jacob is really alone. It is the middle of the night. All his possessions are at the mercy of Esau. He has crossed the stream, moving away from the land God has promised him. He has nothing.

And a man wrestled with him until the breaking of the day (v. 24).

Who is this man, and what is the contest for?

When the man saw that he did not prevail against Jacob, he touched the hollow of his thigh; and Jacob's thigh was put out of joint as he wrestled with him. Then he said, 'Let me go, for the day is breaking.' But Jacob said, 'I will not let you go, unless you bless me.' And he said to him, 'What is your name?' And he said, 'Jacob.' Then he said, 'Your name shall no more be called Jacob, but Israel, for you have striven with God and with men, and have prevailed.' Then Jacob asked him, 'Tell me, I pray, your name.' But he said, 'Why is it that you ask my name?' And he there blessed him. So Jacob called the name of the place Peniel, saying, 'For I have seen God face to face, and yet my life is preserved.' (vv. 25–30)

The most important outcome of the struggle is that Jacob receives the divine blessing. This time it is conferred upon him as he faces God, stripped and alone, not disguised or prey to any plot. Whoever the 'man' is, we can be sure that he is God's agent. He has, therefore, been called an angel (cf. Hos. 12:4). He may be the spirit of the river, a figure who appears in numerous ancient myths; or a spiritual guardian of the lands Jacob is about to enter; or an adversary, roaming to and fro on the earth, as in the book of Job.[5] All the figures may be considered angelic in the terms of the present discussion: threshold spirits under the command of God, who confront people in the path, turning them to a new existence.

Jacob is totally engaged with the angel. Here is no vision, it is a physical contest, the two locked together in the dark. Jacob, who has struggled with Esau even within their mother's womb, is now compelled to wrestle with spiritual power in the form of a man. The term used, translated as 'wrestled', appears nowhere else in the Hebrew Bible. It may have connotations with the word for 'dusty', or possibly the verb 'to embrace'. We might picture a rolling struggle on the ground. Two men are in combat, equally matched; a unique human encounter with God. Yet its very uniqueness is the value of its symbolism. Every single person is called to meet God in the closest possible encounter. Jacob's engagement is a real fight. He gives as good as he gets, so that the spirit begs for release in words that disclose the enigma of its identity. It must be away before the light dawns. Darkness is its covering, mystery its nature. But Jacob demands the blessing which was promised to him, for which he has always striven and is now wounded.

The spirit asks Jacob his name, and then says 'Your name shall no more be called Jacob, but Israel, for you have striven with God and with men, and have prevailed.' The change that is wrought in Jacob in this encounter is more radical than any of the others we have discussed. The change of name brings about a change of persona. He is no longer Jacob, but Israel. This name has no simple interpretation, but could mean one who 'as a prince has power with God', describing Jacob's tenacity and his new, divinely given status. Jacob boldly asks the spirit for his name in exchange. In this respect, however, there is no equality. The angel carries the name of all names, the unnameable, who alone has power to confer blessing. 'And there he blessed him.' The blessing given, the angel's departure is unstated, as sudden and silent as its attack. Jacob knows that he has been wrestling with God. For the third time he stands on holy ground, and must mark it:

> 'So Jacob called the name of the place Peniel ['face of God'], saying, 'For I have seen God face to face, and yet my life is preserved.' The sun rose upon him as he passed Peniel, limping because of his thigh. (vv. 30-31)

The shift in perspective of the narrative is pointed out by Gabriel Josipovici, in his book *The Book of God*:

Without warning we have been moved to a place high above him, looking down on him [Jacob], as, small and defenceless, he limps forward to meet his brother in the light of the newly risen sun . . . Yet this small limping figure is the man who a moment before had seen God face to face, a moment commemorated in the name of the place, which is now, only one verse later, so casually mentioned . . . He is now both more and less than he was before the encounter.[6]

A similar shift in perspective occurs at every human encounter with angels. In the engagement there is a relationship, an exchange in close-up between the two. They inhabit the same world. Then the angel withdraws from sight. For a moment the human seems diminished – perhaps there is a return of the initial fear – then there is movement. The sun rises on Jacob, he walks forward. Nevertheless he bears his injury. He is marked with a visible sign of the angel's effect on him.

> And Jacob lifted up his eyes and looked, and behold, Esau was coming . . .
> But Esau ran to meet him, and embraced him, and fell on his neck and kissed him and they wept. And when Esau raised his eyes and saw the women and children, he said, 'And who are these with you?' Jacob said, 'The children whom God has graciously given your servant.' (33:1 and 4–5)

In the story the wrestling episode has intervened, and with it the blessing. The meeting with Esau is described as though no such intervention has occurred, but we know that Esau's embrace of Jacob embraces a newly blessed, and wounded, Jacob, recently emerged from the divine embrace. Though he is still Jacob, Esau's brother, he has been invested with the name of Israel, by which he bears the whole weight of divine appointment as the father of the chosen race. It will spring from the twelve tribes of his sons. Jacob's answer to Esau's question alludes to this investment and its blessing: his company is the children of Israel, 'the children whom God has graciously given'. Jacob then says to Esau, 'To see your face is like seeing the face of God, with such favour have you received me' (v. 10). The conflict with Esau was resolved in the testing struggle with God. Now Esau can hold no further threat, for the face of God has brought life not death. Jacob allows his brother to think he will follow him south to Esau's land. 'So Esau returned that day on his way to Seir. But Jacob . . . came safely to the city of Shechem which is in the land of Canaan' (vv. 16–18). This is Jacob's final act of guile. He is free to travel northwards across the Jabbok, and then the river Jordan, with all his caravan. Israel has received God's blessing. Later the blessing is ratified, when he returns to Bethel, where he had seen the ladder of angels (see Gen. 35:1–15).

Notes for Part I Chapter 2

1   Peter Levi, from 'The Fox-coloured Pheasant enjoyed his peace', in *The Gravel Ponds* (André Deutsch, London, 1960) p. 23.
2   Gilgal figures in 1 and 2 Samuel, and in 2 Kings, and is referred to by the minor prophets. See also my Part II, chapter 3.
3   In *Gen.* 17:15 God changes the name of Abraham's wife (as he had changed Abram to Abraham) from Sarai to Sarah. 'Sarai' means 'Yah(weh) is prince'; 'Sarah' means 'princess'. 'Abram' means 'Father of height'; 'Abraham' means 'Father of multitudes'.
4   Seamus Heaney, from 'Crossings', in *Seeing Things* (Faber and Faber, London, 1991) p. 85.
5   cf. T. H. Gaster, *Myth, Legend and Custom in the Old Testament* (Harper, London, 1969) pp. 207f., and J. Pedersen, *Israel, its Life and Culture* (Cumberlege, London and Copenhagen, 1926) p. 205. Pedersen maintains that the spirit cannot be an angel of the Lord, *malakh Yahweh*.
6   Gabriel Josipovici, *The Book of God* (Yale University Press, New Haven and London, 1988) pp. 308–9.

3. Are You for Us or for Our Enemies?

That I may rise and stand, o'erthrow me.[1]
(JOHN DONNE)

At the end of his long life, Israel pronounces a prophetic and authoritative blessing upon his grandsons Ephraim and Manasseh, and his son Joseph:

> The God before whom my fathers Abraham and Isaac walked, the God who has led [lit. 'shepherded'] me all my life long to this day, the angel who has redeemed me from all evil, bless the lads; and in them let my name be perpetuated. (Gen. 48:15–16)

Israel refers to the 'angel who has redeemed me from all evil'. He invokes a spirit whose presence, he claims, has saved him from ultimate harm. His life has certainly not been free of evils, but this prayer for the blessing of his grandsons reaches back through all his meetings with the angels of God. He had been assured at Bethel that God would keep him wherever he should go and never leave him, and that the promises would be fulfilled. Jacob first saw angels at Bethel. Twenty years later an angel spoke to him, in the voice of God, telling him to escape from Laban by cunning, and return home with his wives and family. (See Gen. 31:3 and 11–13.) He then saw the army of angels, before wrestling with the spirit by the Jabbok ford. 'The angel who has redeemed me' does not necessarily refer to any of these, but rather to his growing awareness of the presence of God actively 'shepherding' him. This awareness begins at Bethel, is increased with each angelic visitation, until the climax of the naming and blessing at Bethel, and then continues all his life.

Yet that night beside the Jabbok river began with fearful apprehensions, and the spirit who leaped on him in the dark, bringing him to the ground and wounding him when he fought back, did not at first appear to be saving him from harm. Only in the closeness of the struggle did Jacob know that the spirit could bless him; he was compelled to hold on and continue the fight. The scene at the Jabbok ford presents the mediatory nature of angels in another aspect, which appears in other angelic encounters already discussed. The angel with a sword who threatened Balaam, the mysterious man who directed Joseph to his brothers who were plotting to kill him, Moses' divine antagonist at the inn, Jacob's spirit of the night – all these figures display signs of contradiction. Joshua asks the angelic commander: 'Are you for us or for our enemies?' The angels in these scenes appear to be equivocal. They act in an area between light and dark. Their actions may take people through apparent evil into good. The way to God, in these stories, traverses a twilight area where good and evil shift and merge.

In his second letter to the Corinthians Paul describes a situation that complements these texts:

> I know a man in Christ who, fourteen years ago, was caught up – whether still in the body or out of the body, I do not know; God knows – right into the third heaven. I do know, however, that this same person – whether in the body or out of the body, I do not know; God knows – was caught up into paradise and heard things which must not and cannot be put into human language . . . In view of the extraordinary nature of these revelations, to stop me from getting too proud I was given a thorn in the flesh, an angel of Satan to beat me and stop me from getting too proud! About this thing, I have pleaded with the Lord three times to leave me, but he has said, 'My grace is enough for you; my power is at its best in weakness.' So I shall be very happy to make my weakness my

special boast so that the power of Christ may stay over me. (2 Cor. 12:2–4 and 7–9, JB)

Balaam, Joseph, Moses and Jacob could all have become inflated with pride over their particular vision of God and his choice of each of them. The angels rendered them weak; divine power then revealed a new strength under the mark of God's grace. Paul is speaking metaphorically of both the 'thorn' and the 'angel of Satan to beat me'; the latter phrase contains allusions to the Hebrew Bible which evidently helped him to understand his own struggles with God.

We are told that the angel stood in the way 'as his adversary' against Balaam (Num. 22:22). The Hebrew word is *satan*, which appears several times in the Old Testament for personal and national adversaries in general. It can also refer to an anonymous spirit, *hasatan*, 'the adversary', standing in opposition to man, but under the commands of God. This is an ancient tradition. The word 'Satan' was applied much later to the leader of evil spirits. (The verbal root of *satan* may mean something like 'to be remote from', especially from truth, and from the mercy of God.) My present discussion concerns the old tradition of lesser spiritual adversaries.

The adversary in the courts of heaven

In the Hebrew Bible 'the adversary' is no stereotype; it has many different guises. The will of God can be performed by the relatively free actions of insidious spirits. There are three stories where such spirits play a part. Each presents the picture of a divine council chamber, or 'court of heaven'. Such a court, where God presides surrounded by his ministers and attendants, is described by many Old and New Testament prophets and writers, e.g. in Isaiah, Daniel and Psalms, Hebrews and Revelation, etc.

A story in the first book of Kings includes a vision of God's kingly court. It comes in chapter 22, where some false prophets have been persuading Ahab, king of Israel, to fight against the Syrians. They say that God will give him victory. Then Micaiah, a true prophet of God, is called. At first he, too, tells Ahab what the king wants to hear, but Ahab knows well it is not the truth. King Ahab hates Micaiah, who has always prophesied evil concerning the king. However, he presses the prophet to speak the truth, and Micaiah proclaims his vision, like Balaam on the hills with Balak, only here the vision is of Israel defeated and scattered. Micaiah goes on to describe his vision of the court of heaven:

> I saw the Lord sitting on his throne, and all the host of heaven standing beside him on his right hand and on his left; and the Lord said, 'Who will entice Ahab, that he may go up and fall at Ramoth-Gilead?' And one said one thing and another said another. Then a spirit came forward and stood before the Lord, saying, 'I will entice him.' And the Lord said to him, 'By what means?' And he said, 'I will go forth, and will be a lying spirit in the mouth of all his prophets.' And he said, 'You are to entice him, and you shall succeed; go forth and do so.' (1 Kgs 22:19–22)

After he has thrown Micaiah into prison, King Ahab goes into battle at Ramoth-Gilead. He disguises himself, to avoid being killed, but early in the day a chance arrow from the Syrian ranks mortally wounds him. Propped up in his chariot he attempts to deceive both armies into thinking him unharmed and victorious. At sunset he bleeds to death. A cry of defeat is heard, and very soon the Israelite army scatters in confusion. God is not always ready to defend Israel; Ahab has been an evil king and his demise is due. He could have said, with Shakespeare's Macbeth, 'I . . . begin to doubt th'equivocation of the fiend, that lies like truth' (*Macbeth* 5.5, 42–4). Micaiah's vision reveals that the spirits who perform God's will may appear duplicitous at times. Only a true prophet sees through the twilight into the positive darkness of the sovereignty of God.

The Old Testament prophet Zechariah writes of his vision of the night. His fourth vision is of a court scene in

59

heaven. 'The adversary' appears as a prosecutor, and stands up to accuse the Jewish high priest, Joshua (Zech. 3:1f.). We are not told the exact nature of the accusation, but the context is the return of the Jews from exile, where worship of the one true God has been corrupted. The figure of Joshua stands for a new future of Jewish worship with the rebuilding of the temple in Jerusalem. Zechariah sees Joshua dressed in filthy robes which represent both his own sin, and the collective sins of the people. The accusation of the adversary in this scene is a legal formality, but necessary, to point out the wrong. However, the Lord rebukes the satan through the angel who presides over the court, saying:

> 'The Lord who has chosen Jerusalem rebuke you, O Satan; is not this a brand plucked from the fire?' (v. 2)

(It should be noted that *hasatan* is usually translated as 'Satan' in English Bibles. In order to avoid confusion between the two different traditions which I have indicated, I shall write 'the satan' here, and in my subsequent discussion of the book of Job.)

> And the angel said to those who were standing before him, 'Remove the filthy garments from him,' and to Joshua he said, 'Behold I have taken your iniquity away from you, and I will clothe you in rich apparel.' And I [Zechariah] said, 'Let them put a clean turban on his head.' So they put a clean turban on his head and clothed him with garments, and the angel of the Lord was standing by. And the angel of the Lord enjoined Joshua, 'Thus says the Lord of Hosts; if you will walk in my ways and keep my charge, then you shall rule my house and have charge of my courts.' (vv. 4–7)

Joshua's guilt is symbolically removed. Moses, too, after the accuser has sought to kill him, was symbolically exonerated.

The satan of Zechariah's vision is a prosecutor who stands over against God, but is not set in full opposition. He is only a part of the fulfilment of God's mandate. He is not even allowed to reply, when the angel of the Lord stands up for the high priest, his 'brand plucked from the fire'. Joshua is scorched and blackened, but will be ritually cleansed.

The book of Job presents another image of the satan as an accuser, in its opening chapters. This story, more than any other, tells of the absolute mystery of God's purpose. After introducing Job, blameless and God-fearing, the scene moves to the court of heaven:

> Now there was a day when the sons of God came to present themselves before the Lord, and the satan among them. (1:6)

God presides over his spiritual councillors. The term 'sons of God' [lit. 'sons of the gods'] is used frequently in Hebrew to describe superhuman beings. The adversary is among them.

> The Lord said to the satan, 'Whence have you come?' The satan answered the Lord, 'From going to and fro on the earth, and from walking up and down on it.' (v. 7)

Not only has the adversary been roaming about, but all the 'sons of the gods' have evidently come to God's court from elsewhere. (In Zechariah's first vision he is told by an angel that some mysterious horsemen are 'they whom the Lord has sent to patrol the earth': Zech. 1:10). The adversary, however, has been taking note of human behaviour:

> And the Lord said to the satan, 'Have you considered my servant Job, that there is none like him on the earth, a blameless and upright man, who fears God and turns away from evil?' Then the satan answered the Lord, 'Does Job fear God for nought? Hast thou not put a hedge about him and his house and all that he has, on every side? Thou hast blessed the work of his hands, and his possessions have increased in the land. But put forth thy hand now, and touch all that he has, and he will curse

thee to thy face.' And the Lord said to the satan, 'Behold, all that he has is in your power; only upon himself do not put forth your hand.' So the satan went forth from the presence of the Lord. (vv. 8–12)

The adversary is permitted to express his opinion, the cynical scepticism of which prompts a further licence from God, that he may put it to the test. From whose 'hand' will the misfortune come? The satan's suggestion is that God will act; God gives the adversary a conditional freedom of action. The narrator leaves the question unanswered, for when the disasters fall upon Job the scene is set squarely on earth, so that the reader sees with the eyes of Job who has no knowledge of the conversation in heaven. (It is worth noting, however, that the events are told as though they were what are legally known as 'acts of God'.) Job does not fail the test. Chapter 2 returns to the celestial court, exactly as before. The Lord points out Job's resistance:

'He still holds fast his integrity, although you moved me against him, to destroy him without cause.' The satan answered the Lord, 'Skin for skin! All that a man has he will give for his life. But put forth thy hand now and touch his bone and his flesh and he will curse thee to thy face.' And the Lord said to the satan, 'Behold, he is in your power; only spare his life.' (2:3–6)

Again God sets limits on the adversary. This time we are told who performs the deed:

So the satan went forth from the presence of the Lord, and afflicted Job with loathsome sores from the sole of his foot to the crown of his head (v. 7).

After this the adversary disappears from the narrative. Job is never informed of the part it played.

The mystery of God's ways

In the following thirty-six chapters of the book, Job and his family and friends discuss why he should be thus afflicted. Finally, in chapter 38, God speaks 'out of the whirlwind'. The image is not only a poetical device, for the answer God gives to Job is framed as an exposition of the mysteries of creation. In a long series of rhetorical questions God makes it plain to Job that the ways of the Creator are far beyond the comprehension of his creatures, even rational man. 'God shows him how little he knows of the structure of the universe; the beautiful ebbing and flowing of the dance of creation.'[2]

> 'Where were you when I laid the foundation of the earth? Tell me, if you have understanding.
> Who determined its measurements – surely you know!
> Or who stretched the line upon it?
> On what were its bases sunk, or who laid its cornerstone,
> When the morning stars sang together,
> And all the sons of the gods shouted for joy?'
>
> (38:4–7)

The poem then moves freely across the categories of sea, sky, earth and living creatures. All are enigmatic, and far from any supposed mastery of human beings. The satan's reasoning at the very beginning of the book of Job is part of overall creaturely ignorance; the adversary asserted that Job's prosperity was the sole foundation of his fidelity, but is proved wrong. We are reminded of Jesus' reply to Peter when he tried to reason: 'The way you think is not God's way, but man's'[3] (Matt. 16:23). Paul said that his 'angel of satan' was sent in order to prevent him becoming puffed up with pride over his mystical experience. In saying this he presumes a knowledge of cause and effect, according to his own logic. In fact he could never know the true reasons for his suffering; they remain hidden in God. The answer to his prayer for the 'thorn' to be removed is simply 'My grace is sufficient for you.'

Job's anguish is converted to surrender upon his experience of God himself:

> 'I had heard of thee by the hearing of the ear,
> but now my eye sees thee;
> therefore I despise myself,
> and repent in dust and ashes.'
>
> (42:5–6)

In his book *Das Heilige* Rudolph Otto points out that Job is not only silenced by his perception of the Lord, he also finds peace. It is 'an appeasement which would alone and in itself perfectly suffice as the solution of the problem of the book of Job, even without Job's rehabilitation in the closing verses'.[4] What Job perceives is not a rational conclusion of any kind. The effect upon him cannot be rendered in terms of a conclusion at all, even as broadly as saying that Job stood a test of fidelity to God's will. In the last resort, the theodicy of The book of Job, in chapters 38–41, presents the divine mystery in its totally non-rational form. 'We have,' writes Rudolph Otto, 'the element of the mysterious displayed in rare purity and completeness, and these chapters may well rank among the most remarkable in the history of religion.' In them the creation is shown to be inexplicable, even purposeless. Job bows before the utter mysteriousness of God in his majesty and transcendence. Such an acknowledgement enables him to transcend himself and his suffering, and he finds peace.

The function of all the adverse spirits we have studied is to facilitate the revelation of truth. Moving in the shadows, they are nevertheless mediators between God and humanity. They number among the hosts of angels, like those revealed to Gehazi as chariots of fire, who are for us rather than against us. The later Old Testament texts, such as Zechariah and Job, present the adversary with more character than the equivocal spirits of the earlier writings, but its role is clearly in a different mode from that of the subsequently named Satan, Prince of evil. In Zechariah, written about 520 BC, the high priest's accuser is a silent presence, something of a legal formality, but the reaction to its accusation is written in colourful language, charged with feeling. The adversary evokes an emotional response. Job was written about a hundred years later. There the satan shows an almost Miltonic bearing.[5] He is a cynical, lone observer. His speech has insolence and wit. While his powers are limited, he is responsible for the most horrible of Job's sufferings. Having produced his effect, he disappears from the story, and the final outcome proves him to have been merely an instrument. Paul's metaphorical use of the term 'angel of Satan' acknowledges the old Hebrew tradition of the adversary as just such an instrument of the divine purpose. He enters the story of Job among the sons of the gods, and leaves it trailing disaster. In the disaster, however, Job finally knows God.

Notes for Part I Chapter 3

[1] John Donne, 'Holy Sonnets'.
[2] Angela Tilby, *Science and the Soul* (SPCK, London, 1992) p. 184.
[3] Jerusalem Bible translation, which is nearer to the Greek than RSV in this line.
[4] Rudolph Otto, *Das Heilige*, translated by J. W. Harvey as *The Idea of the Holy* (O.U.P., Oxford, 1923; Penguin Books, Harmondsworth, 1959) p. 23.
[5] I have not quoted from Milton at all, since I feel the angels in *Paradise Lost* are far too human to be useful examples of spiritual beings.

4. Order

Where were you when I laid the
foundation of the earth? . . .
When the morning stars sang together,
and all the sons of God shouted for joy?

(JOB 38:4 AND 7)

God asks Job what he thinks he can possibly know about
creation and its complexities; was he there when its measurements were determined? He was not, but when those first
stars 'sang together' the 'sons of God shouted for joy'. This
poem in Job suggests that angels witnessed the creation of the
stars by God, and expressed their delight. The only other
Biblical text that refers to the angels' origins is Psalm 104,
which describes God's majesty in the universe he has made,
and the order in which he made it – a similar order to that in
Genesis 1. In the psalm the angels, 'messengers' and 'ministers' (v. 4), are made before the earth is set on its foundations.
Many of the fourth-century Christian Fathers speculated
about the exact point at which the angels were created in the
coming-to-be of the universe. Because angels do not figure in
the creation myth of the opening chapters of Genesis, a place
had to be found for them, it seems. Augustine said the angels
were created with the first light, on the first day. 'God said,
"Let there be light"; and there was light' (Gen. 1:3). Augustine
takes the verse from Job as his justification: if the angels
rejoiced when the stars were made, i.e. on the fourth day, then
they themselves were made before that day, and since they
are not mentioned on the third or second days, they must have
been in that first light. They immediately became, said
Augustine, 'partakers of the eternal light which is the
unchanging wisdom of God, of John 1:9.'[1]

The early Fathers based their theories of the creation of

angels upon the accepted dualistic thinking that was preva-
lent for many centuries. Spirit and body, or matter, were
considered to be entirely separate entities. If angels are spiritual, as opposed to bodily, beings, then their creation falls
into place before the creation of matter, while 'the earth was
without form, and void'. Origen in the third century said, 'all
souls and spirits were created before the material world'
(human souls being held in God until they inhabit a body).[2]
In the fourth century Basil, Gregory Nazianzen, Ambrose
and Hilary all advocated the pre-existence of angels to the
rest of the universe, and John Cassian in the fifth century
stated categorically: 'None of the faithful doubts that angels
were created before visible matter.'[3]

As well as belief in angels as non-corporeal beings, the
factor of time came into the question. Spirits exist beyond
time, but not in eternity which is proper to God alone, it was
said. The term 'aeon' was used for a period before the creation
of time; having a beginning it is commensurable with time,
but outside it. According to Basil, it was in this extra-
temporal condition that God created the angelic world.[4]
Thomas Aquinas, the thirteenth-century theologian, used a
similar terminology with regard to the angels and time.[5] But
in answer to the question 'were angels created before the
physical universe?' he answered that angels and corporeal
creatures were created simultaneously. 'For the angels are
part of the universe, in the sense that they do not constitute
a universe of their own, but are combined with the physical
creation to form one total world.'[6] The Lateran Council had
stated, not long before, that 'God, from the beginning of time,
had made at once (*simul*) out of nothing both orders of creatures, the spiritual and the corporeal.' (See my Introduction,
p. 14.) As far as the time of their creation is concerned, in his
answer Aquinas directs the reader to a more valuable line of
thought: the angels are combined with the physical universe
to form 'one total world'. Nothing could be more modern, now,
than the concept of one total world, the interrelation of every
part of the universe. Aquinas was not, of course, describing
a total physical universe such as we understand today. He

was thinking rather of the final purpose, or end, of the universe, every part of which God has ordered for his ultimate glory.[7]

The question of when the angels were created is not really an issue nowadays. We are perhaps more inclined to see the creation of angels as part of ongoing creation; God, who goes on working (cf. John 5:17), continues to create – angels, men and women, and all the complexities of the universe – while time lasts. The poetry of the Genesis myth, and God's exhortation of Job, continue to take their place as ways of expressing God's mysterious creatorship, alongside changing theories of the origins of the universe produced by cosmologists. Augustine's idea that the angels are partakers of the eternal light which is the unchanging wisdom of God can also serve our imaginations and our faith as we read the first verses of John's Gospel. About the angels' origins only the poet or myth-maker can frame an account.

When Aquinas wrote of 'one total world' he went on to say that this totality, or interrelationship, is apparent from the 'ordering of one creature to another. Indeed the order of things to one another is to the universal good.'[8] The 'order of things', *ordo rerum*, was seen, in the Middle Ages particularly, as a systematic chain. The medieval conception of the world was derived from a mixture of Platonism and Judaic Christianity with centuries of theorizing on the structure of an ordered universe arranged hierarchically. In its simplest terms the hierarchy consists of basic 'matter' at the bottom of the scale, through to inert things such as rocks, above which is the vegetable kingdom, then the sensitive life of animals, then humankind who, living both by the senses and the intellect, stands at the highest point of the material world. Above humankind is the non-material intellectual world of spirits, to which the human intellect can aspire. This was said to be the natural order; angels are natural because created. The only supernatural realm is that of God himself. When Aquinas was writing about angels in his theological treatises he set out the subject as a discussion of the differences between the human and angelic naturs. He also attempted to describe the difference of the angelic nature from that of God. In both cases he pointed out the limitations of the former compared with the latter. Since angels were believed to be pure intellects (though not all theologians agreed with this), Aquinas placed them in a realm between humanity and God. If there were no such realm a gap would appear in the chain, or order, of being: because God (at the very top of the chain) causes, or creates, by his intellect and will, it follows that the universe would be incomplete without creatures of pure intellect, having no need of bodily senses.[9]

Aquinas and others have tried to reach conclusions about the angels' nature which place them securely in this transcendency, between us and God. In doing so they have at times so rarefied angels that our experience cannot touch them. It is easy to get lost in the fine details of speculation on angelic intellect and will, even though Aquinas refers frequently to the Bible, and does not deviate from his own clear and systematic reasoning. (The over-used example of an argument over the maximum number of angels able to dance on a pinhead is not only apocryphal – it appears in no medieval text – but misrepresents a valid area of discussion about number and infinity.) However his thought relies on the hypothesis that angels are non-corporeal, pure spirit. We no longer see body and soul as separate; such dualism now seems untenable, and to categorize angels as bodiless spirits tells us very little, though the argument appealed to the medieval mind.

Aquinas, in tune with the thinking of his day, laboured much over definitions of angelic potentiality. It may well be that angels have differing powers; in the Bible this is apparent, but can we with any certainty classify these degrees of power? Karl Rahner warns against possible dangers in studying angels, one of which is 'an excessive concern for facile orderliness'.[10] He has in mind the systems, widely accepted in the Middle Ages, which have formed the basis of over-simplified notions of angelic degree and function. These systems take their origin chiefly from the sixth-century theologian Dionysius,[11] who was highly regarded by Aquinas writing six hundred years later.

The angelic hierarchy of Dionysius

Dionysius sets out nine orders of angels, taking their titles from Old and New Testament terminology. Knowledge of these ranks was commonplace until only recently, entering into literature and folklore. 'Nine for the nine bright shiners', we still sing, in 'Green grow the rushes, O', but the reference will largely pass unrecognized now. The Church embraced Dionysius' system in many of its writings, and at times his names and ranks were taught. As a result angels have, for some people, been merely a list of incomprehensible names, whose order they could not remember accurately, and who bore no real relation to everyday life. But the reduction of Dionysius' work to a mere catalogue is a travesty. It stands in its rightful place in the history of philosophy and theology, and should be read according to the lights of its own age. There is much in what he said that can assist our understanding of angelic power, by imagery and insight, but its elaborate and exact details cannot be accepted now, any more than his philosophical foundation can be used to define reality.

In principle Dionysius describes a scheme of angelic interaction determined by the Neo-Platonic theory of emanation. Using the image of light, God is understood to pour forth his divine ray, which is received by those beings whose created perfection places them nearest to him. Their contemplation enables them to reflect the light of God and again pour it forth upon those below them, like mirrors angled to the sun. Every order receives the light exactly according to its own capacity, and is perfected by it. Lifted to the ultimate point of its degree, it meets with the grade above, and at the same time bestows the light upon those below, that they may be likewise raised. Thus all the goodness of God is imparted to his creatures, and draws them to him.

Dionysius constructs his systems in threes, through all

his writings. He sees the universe, at every level, as formed in triads which are themselves unities, and which connect with other monadic triads related to them. In this Dionysius describes the world as a reflection of the Holy Trinity, God who is Three and One. At the same time he follows Plato, whose philosophy is Dionysius' guiding light, as reinterpreted by the Neo-Platonists of his own day. Plato had also used a triadic construction in his description of the universe. Dionysius' attempts to understand angelic motivation tackle the fundamental question of unity and diversity, which is: how does the One give rise to the many and remain One, and how do the many return to the One? Dionysius' *Celestial Hierarchy* proposes a system that demonstrates this process in action. He brings it right down to earth, saying that the hierarchy of heavenly beings is reflected in ecclesiastical and civil hierarchies, which he again groups in threes; these are in turn reflected in the laws of nature. In yet other writings he works out another reflection, within each human soul which may ascend by threefold stages to eventual perfect union with God.[12] For we can only be truly enlightened by the Divine radiance itself, says Dionysius.[13] The scale of angelic hierarchies can lead our minds towards that simplicity, and through the angels we can actually strive towards it. He insists that any concrete images he employs are symbols, to help us perceive the spiritual life of angels. He does not suggest that the angels really are fire or thrones etc.; the very use of such base symbols, he says, underlines the fact that the angels are far beyond them (ch. 2).

The nine orders of angels are arranged in groups of three. The first group consists of Seraphim, Cherubim and Thrones. (In spite of his disclaimers over the use of symbols, once Dionysius is in his stride, describing and naming the ranks of angels, he never suggests that these names and attributes are arbitrarily selected; all is presented as reality, justified by Biblical quotations interpreted in his own way.) The Seraphim, who are closest to God, are all fire and movement as they receive the most pure light from God and pass it on, kindling those immediately below them. These are the

Cherubim, possessing a power of knowing and receptivity that enables them to be filled with the light and in turn pour it out. The Thrones are fully and perfectly established in power; they receive without passion or impurity the Divine Immanence from above. These three form one group whose work is to participate in and impart the highest mystery of pure light (ch. 7).

The middle orders are the Dominions, Virtues and Powers (*kyrioteton, dunameon, exousion*). The Dominions are true lords; they have unbounded elevation to that which is above, freedom from any inconsistency, fullness of purpose. Under them the Virtues ascend with unshakeable strength, and abundantly fill with virtue those below, the Powers. Co-equal with the Dominions and Virtues, these exhibit a perfect regulation of supermundane authority, beneficently leading those beneath them. This group is purified and illuminated by the group above, but receive a less resplendent light. They are communicators of Truth (ch. 8).

The lowest group is made up of Principalities, Archangels and Angels. Their leaders are wholly turned towards the Prince of Princes (Christ), and with a godlike authority initiate the others in princely powers. The Archangels, occupying the middle position of this triad, are the cause of union of the Angels with the Principalities, their own lordship. This is the interpreting order. It receives and hands on the illuminations reflected from above. The Angels fill up and complete the lowest rank, so they are most properly called Angels by us, because their rank is directly in contact with the world. This triad is the revealing order, and they preside over the human hierarchies (ch. 9). Dionysius says that all the ranks are called celestial powers, but the characteristics of the higher must not be assigned to the lower, or order is destroyed (ch. 11).

Dionysius clings to the notion that a turning upwards is essential to the proper life and action of each angelic order. They do not receive the light of God except from the order directly above them, nor do they mediate it to any other except the order below. Thomas Aquinas did not accept that the angels' knowledge of God derives from their contact with the immediately higher angels, or that their receptivity is entirely in this relation. 'All the angels,' says Aquinas, 'higher as well as lower, see God's essence without any medium.'[14] The grace of God must have an immediacy of power and communication that will by-pass any order.

Dionysius' scale is, of course, imaged in Jacob's vision of the ladder of angels ascending and descending between heaven and earth. But the accent on light in Dionysius' work is perhaps its most valuable teaching. It is in tune with the Bible, where light is a primary image of God and his self-revelation. Augustine's suggestion, already quoted, that angels at their creation were 'partakers of the eternal light which is the unchanging wisdom of God', leads into the Dionysian system. It is not hard to accept the idea that one of the angels' chief functions is to shine that light into the world. In the Bible angels are frequently described as 'shining' or 'luminous'. They are often signalled by fire, as with the chariots above Dothan. Some have speculated that their actual substance is light. A Jewish tradition states that they are composed of an 'ethereal fiery matter, a blazing light'.[15] We will meet many more instances of the images of fire and light in connection with angels in the course of this book. Dionysius has developed what is undoubtedly a true aspect of angelic nature and substance into an over-regimented system of the transmission of the unearthly light down through the ranks. In one way it demonstrates how far our knowledge of light must be from Divine Light, but nevertheless that Light is available directly to us, as well as to the 'Seraphim'. Angels may be mediators of it in all sorts of ways, and they may carry it as an attribute of angelic existence, but I doubt if we should try to assess how much of it one angel might be endowed with, or exactly how it may be imparted to the world.

Angels in relation to order

The hierarchy of angels was a way of expressing in figures and symbols what is beyond human understanding, as

Dionysius declared. It appealed to the medieval mind. The bases for theories of order in the universe are entirely different now, but nevertheless the existence of order is rarely denied by either scientists or philosophers. Order is found in all our experience, and may – in part or perhaps wholly – be created by us in our grasp of that experience. As we see it, God is unquestionably 'higher' than we are, and if we believe in spiritual power created by him and working for him, then we will assuredly put that power 'above' our own powers. We experience a common human desire to 'rise' beyond our limitations in understanding and achievements. We are drawn to the transcendent; from the finite to the infinite, the temporal to the eternal, the transient to the unchanging, by fundamental tendencies of human nature. Angels may be assisting us towards these things, which Christians believe are found by drawing nearer to God. Nowadays we would see the orderliness of angels as stemming from a condition in which every part stands in proper relation to the whole. As part of creation the angels stand in an essential relationship to the matter of the world, and the unity of the cosmos, including its component of human experience throughout time. The ontology of angels can only be studied through this network of relation, which itself bears relation to God.

The Bible has no systematic ordering of angels. Even in the book of Revelation their range cannot be analysed with any precision. John, too, has expressed his vision in images which relate to the traditions of his time. One of those traditions was in similar vein to Dionysius' plan but in no way so rigid: that a number of angels are privileged to stand close to the throne of God. These angels were known as 'the angels of the presence'. In Revelation John makes reference to 'seven angels who stand before God' (8.2). Some commentators identify John's seven with the 'Seven Archangels' of later Jewish writings. The word 'archangel' appears only twice in the Bible, in the New Testament (1 Thess. 4:16 and Jude v. 9). The term was developed in later Jewish angelology, and the names of the seven varied from writer to writer. The three names that appear fairly consistently are Gabriel, Raphael and Michael. These names have been taken up by the Christian Church as credible identities, since they all figure, separately, in the scriptural canon. The names of the three 'archangels' may be seen as valid symbols, the figures of these angels being held to represent groups of angels with particular functions, as we see them in action in the Bible texts. Gabriel is directly concerned with the mystery of the incarnation. He is 'messenger' *par excellence* (see my Part II). Raphael's identity has no such clear stamp, but his role in the book of Tobit has led him to be associated with the ministry of guardian angels, and his name bears relation to healing (see Part III). Michael, in the three Biblical references to him, is engaged in the battle against evil, on behalf of humankind. He figures in revelations of the final perfection of the kingdom of God (see Part IV). But, before these three 'orders' of angelic ministry, another group of angels demands attention: the evil angels against which Michael is seen to battle at the end of the world.

Notes for Part I Chapter 4

[1] *De Civitate Dei* XI, ix.
[2] *De Principiis* I, vii.
[3] *Collationes* VIII, vii.
[4] *In Hexaemaron* hom. I, v.
[5] *Summa Theologica* Ia, X, v. 'The aeon is a term derived by a different route from the same word as "eternity". In the early years of Greek philosophy it was in use as a measure of duration, which became distinct from eternity strictly so-called. Lucretius, the early Gnostics and the neo-Platonists all make use of the term.' T. McDermott OP, in the Blackfriars edition of *Summa Theologica* Vol. 2, p. 147.
[6] *Summa Theologica* Ia, LXI, iii, trans. Kenelm Foster OP.
[7] *Summa Contra Gentiles* III, xvii–xxii.
[8] *Summa Theologica* Ia, LXI, iii.
[9] ibid. Ia, L, i.

[10] *Concise Theological Dictionary* (London, 1965).

[11] Dionysius, known as the 'pseudo-Areopagite', is believed to have lived around AD 500, in Syria. For nearly a thousand years the writings of this Dionysius were attributed to Paul's Athenian convert of Acts 17:34. He was probably a pupil of Proclus or his successor, Damascius, who were neo-Platonist philosophers. Dionysius' writings are a synthesis of Christian dogma with neo-Platonist thought. He wrote in Greek, but his works were best known in the Latin translations of John Scotus Erigena in the ninth century.

[12] I refer to Dionysius' treatise *Mystical Theology*, which had an enormous influence on medieval writings about mystical prayer. From him came valuable insights into the need for a process of 'unknowing' in our personal approach to God.

The titles of all Dionysius' works are as follows:

The Celestial Hierarchy (peri tes ouranias hierarchias)
The Ecclesiastical Hierarchy (peri tes ecclesiastikes hierarchias)
The Divine Names (peri theion onamaton)
Mystical Theology (peri mustikes theologias) ed. J. P. Migne, *Patrologia Graeca* 3 and 4.

[13] *Celestial Hierarchy* 1.

[14] *Summa Theologica* Ia, CVI, i.

[15] Midrash Tehillim on Psalm 104:4 quoted in G. Moore, *Judaism* (Cambridge University Press, Cambridge, 1975) p. 405.

5. Disorder

They have neither knowledge nor understanding,
they walk about in darkness;
all the foundations of the earth are shaken.

I say, 'You are gods,
sons of the Most High, all of you;
nevertheless, you shall die like men,
and fall like any prince.'
(Ps. 82:5–7)

The 'order' of angels can be seen best as a condition of proper relation, rather than a list of categories. That proper relation is part of the indescribably complex web of the universe, but its simplest aspect is the angels' relation to God. From that come all other connections between them and creation. The adversaries we considered in chapter 3 maintained their relation to God, and assisted, though subversively, to bring certain people into better relation with God. The stories were mostly from the Old Testament; in the New Testament the adversary takes on a different aspect altogether. He is called 'the Devil', *ho diabolos*, or 'Satan'. He appears as a personal being, in opposition to God and to Christ. The root meaning of *diabolos* suggests the opposite of *symbollein*: rather than bringing things together, he is defined as taking things apart; the Devil is an anti-symbol. As a prime adversary, Satan obstructs the way to God. He is described as the leader of an army of evil spirits who are blamed for a great many of the disasters and ills of the world.

More has been written about the Devil and demons than about angels, yet there is as much scepticism about their reality. Since we recognize in ourselves a propensity for evil that appears, mostly, greater or stronger than our propensity for good, many people consider the power of evil to be purely subjective: there is, they consider, no actual evil power outside the human will. All the evil in the world, in this case, comes about through the perversities of humankind. In the Bible, and in nearly all religious traditions, evil is incurred both through human misdoing and through the actions of spiritual powers that are opposed to good. Now, if there really are such spirits whose motivation is evil, how did they come into being? Judaism and Christianity hold that God is absolute Being, absolute Good, and can therefore have no opposite. So the power of evil has no equality of power with God, in Judaeo-Christian faith. If there are evil spirits, they are created by God, the creator of everything, and since all that God creates is good, evil spirits must have turned from good to evil. Thomas Aquinas, in making this point, refers to the heresy of the Manichaeans, arising in the third century, who said that Satan's very nature was evil from its origins. For them the division of light and darkness had existed as separate cosmic principles from the beginning of the universe, darkness being the source of evil.

Light and darkness are certainly basic symbols of good and evil, and by analogy are helpful in understanding that to the religious believer evil cannot be absolute: in the same way that darkness exists only as an absence of light, so evil is only the absence of good. Darkness is always dispelled by light, never the other way round. The presence of evil in the world is always under the power of God's comprehensive good. An evil spirit cannot have equality of power with the spirits whose purpose is to mediate the Good. Nevertheless the power of evil is undoubtedly strong; questions about its source and potential must be addressed, difficult though it is to find satisfactory answers. It is not my purpose to discuss the philosophy or theology of the problem of evil, but to consider the possible nature and activities of evil spirits in opposition to angels. We cannot be sure of their existence, any more than that of angels, but by looking at passages in the New Testament, some beliefs about them may be clarified.

Lucifer and the fallen angels

In Christianity the Devil's loss of a nature that was created good is explained as a 'fall'. 'I saw Satan fall like lightning from heaven,' Jesus said (Luke 10:18). The concept of the Devil as a fallen angel, and of all evil spirits as having also fallen, is common to all Semitic peoples. These spirits were seen as accursed gods or demons, punished for sinning against their divine nature, and thrust out of heaven. The Fathers of the Christian Church took a passage from Isaiah as a parable of the fall of Satan. The use of this passage has resulted in the prince of evil angels being also called 'Lucifer'. The name means 'light-bearer', and was taken up after it appeared in Jerome's Latin Bible of the fourth century AD:

> Quomodo cecidisti de caelo, Lucifer, qui mane oriebaris?
> (How are you fallen from heaven, Lucifer, who once did herald the dawn?) (Isaiah 14:12, my translation)

The Hebrew may be translated:

> How are you fallen from heaven, Helel ben Shahar!

The name Helel ben Shahar is scornfully applied by the writer to the King of Babylon in prophecy, or perhaps to the fallen tyrant Sargon of Assyria. *Helel ben Shahar* means 'shining son of the dawn' (hence Jerome's Latin translation) and comes from an ancient non-Israelite myth of a god who aspired to ascend the mountain of gods and make himself equal to the High God, for which presumption he was cast down into the nether world.[1] Christian writers supposed the 'Light-Bearer' to have been a principal angel, perhaps the highest angel of all. Its fall is consequently great, and from being a Prince of Light, Lucifer or Satan became the Prince of Darkness.

The myth of Satan's fall has naturally entailed speculation as to the nature of the sin that caused it. Some of this speculation follows the line of the ancient stories: it was a desire to be equal with God – in other words, pride. Guesswork of this kind leads to a multiplicity of legends, rather than an approach to truth. We cannot know what caused these angels to fall from grace, but that very phrase is perhaps the best clue. Somehow evil angels have forfeited the gift of Grace, the gift that enables God's creatures to enter into relation with God. Some say Satan, or Lucifer, as a leading angel, was followed in his fall by a number of subservient angels. It seems more possible that each 'fallen' angel is responsible for its own demise. In trying to imagine how this could have happened, some aspects of the nature of all angels must come under consideration. In the notes to his edition of Aquinas' *Summa Theologica*, Kenelm Foster OP suggests that if, as Aquinas says, the angelic nature is a totality in itself, when it makes a choice its choice is complete. If an angel decides either for-God or against-God the choice involves the very self of the angel; it has no half-measures. Its choice *is* itself. So for an angel to decide against God entails a removal from God affecting the very nature of the angel. This is another guess, but a plausible one. The nature of such an angel is no longer in order, in proper relation to God. It is disordered, and will cause disorder in its every action.

'I saw Satan fall like lightning from heaven.' These words, in their context in Luke's Gospel, ch. 10, proclaim the eternal past, present and future of Satan's fall: the original defection, the constant putting down of evil by those who serve God (in this case it is the seventy disciples who have been given power 'to tread upon serpents and scorpions, and over all the power of the enemy', v. 19) and the eventual defeat through Christ's death, resurrection and eternal glory. The disciples were told to look towards that final victory, in which they were chosen to share, rather than the minor victories along the way (v. 20). 'For as the lightning comes from the east and shines as far as the west, so will be the coming of the Son of Man' (Matt. 24:27). Jesus Christ 'came down from heaven' so that he might take the whole human race 'up to heaven' to live with him in God. 'For our sake he made him to be sin who knew no sin, so that in him we might become the righteousness of God' (2 Cor. 5:21). In 'coming down' Christ has counteracted the outcome of the 'fall' of Satan. In the Gospels we read how Satan tried to retaliate by tempting Jesus (Matt. 4:1–11; Mark 1:12–13; Luke 4:1–13). Jesus was tempted, humanly, to decide for himself how to conduct his mission, to achieve his status. In a section of his novel *The Brothers Karamazov*, Dostoevsky expounds on the possible consequence of Jesus accepting the Devil's offers, thereby winning humanity to himself by overt miracles: turning stones into bread so that there would be no hunger in the world; revealing his divinity in ways that would appeal to human comprehension at its lowest. In Ivan Karamazov's parable the Grand Inquisitor, who is offering Jesus a second chance, says to Jesus: 'Did you forget that man prefers peace, and even death, to freedom of choice in the knowledge of good and evil?'[2] Dostoevsky explores the cunning of the Devil's exploitation of human weakness, as against true freedom offered by God in Christ, which, as we know, entails the risk of faith. The Gospels tell how Satan offered to change places with Christ; Jesus could have dominion in the world, if he reinstated this fallen spirit, and worshipped it as a god. But Jesus knew how narrow worldly dominion would be. The Devil desired to see the Son of God fall from heaven, but Christ turned his eyes on him in full recognition of this subtle inversion of reality. He reminded Satan whom he was addressing: 'You shall not tempt the Lord your God.'

Evil angels in the world

In John's Gospel Satan is three times referred to as the 'ruler' or 'prince, of this world' (12:31; 14:30; 16:11). John favours the word *kosmos*; Paul often uses *aiōnos*, e.g. 'the rulers of this age' in 1 Corinthians 2:8. In all cases the accent should fall on 'world' rather than on 'ruler', and perhaps from this we can say that Satan does not control the world, but rather that his power is confined to it, in time. The temporal cosmos is the only field of operation for Satan and his followers. They are no longer mediators; they have forfeited the right to move between earth and heaven, to work in time out of eternity. Their actions are not ordered towards the new earth and the new heaven of eternity, they are disordered, limited to what is passing away and has no future. The Devil is the prince of death, (cf. Heb. 2:14 and Rev. 6:8) that is, death as finality. He rules only, in the world, over those who see it as an end in itself, choosing to confine themselves to it.

I have said that Satan is 'confined' to this world; he is 'limited' to its mortality. The vocabulary expresses constriction, as opposed to enlargement. The action of evil angels is bounded by the finite, they are denied the freedom that is open to infinity through growth and true development. Like the Smallweed family in Dickens' novel *Bleak House*, with no children growing up, and stunted like Grandfather Smallweed, their every tendency is to thwart and restrict. Because the evil angels have turned away from God into themselves, as it were, they can only move towards further compression, like an astral 'black hole'. Jesus felt the constriction of mortality upon him; he had to suffer it, though he held the whole power of immortality. 'I have a baptism to be baptized with, and how I am constrained (*synechomai*) until it is accomplished!' (Luke 12:50). Finite creation was given freedom from mortal constraint through God's taking on its mortality in Christ. The death of Christ was at the same time his submission to the world as subject to death, and his triumph in bringing it through death into eternal life with him. As he approached his crucifixion Christ proclaimed, according to John's Gospel: 'Now is the judgement of this world, now shall the ruler of this world be cast out' (12:31). By lifting all people up with him, he raised us above the dead-end place where Satan is coiled. As he came nearer to death he felt the Devil drawing closer; 'I will no longer talk much with you, for the ruler of this world is coming. He has no power over me . . .' Christ contains heaven, where Satan is powerless. 'But I do as the Father has commanded me, so that the world may know that I love the

Father' (John 14:30–1). Jesus submitted himself in free will to darkness. Entering the darkness he proved its negativity in the light of love. The coming of the Holy Spirit, who is that light, made it clear that the ruler of this world is already judged (John 16:11).

Because they were mystified by him, some people accused Jesus of casting out demons through the power of the Devil, of 'Beelzebul', a Hebrew name of mixed origins for a principal evil spirit. (The form 'Beelzebub' is a contemptuous play on words to make 'Lord of the flies'.) Their accusation was illogical, as Jesus pointed out: 'If Satan is divided against himself, how will his kingdom stand?' It is by the 'finger of God' whose kingdom is infinitely stronger than Satan's, that the Devil is not only defeated, but bound within his own house. In Luke the parable shows Satan stripped of his armour and with his spoils divided. The image of division and disintegration is carried into Jesus' next words: 'He who does not gather with me, scatters' (Luke 11:14–23). The actions of Satan are passing, dissolute; they are 'like chaff which the wind drives away' (Ps. 1:4).

There is a distinction between 'practising' evil and 'doing' good. This is brought out clearly in two places in John's Gospel. The translators have not been careful enough to mark this important difference:

John 3:20–1: The one practising [Greek *prasson*] evil things [*phaula*] hates the light . . . but the one doing [*poion*] the truth comes into the light.
John 5:29: Those having done [*poisantes*] good things will come forth into the resurrection of life, and those having practised [*praxantes*] evil things to the resurrection of judgement. (My translation)

The Greek *poiein* means both 'to make' and 'to do', and carries a creative significance. *Prassein* on the other hand is simply the act: 'He who practises has nothing but his *pragma*, which is an event, a thing of the past, a source to him only of condemnation, for he has nothing to show for it, and it is also worthless (the meaning of *phaula*); whereas he who makes has his *poiema* (the thing made), he has abiding fruit. The expressions will not admit of interchange.'[3] By this token Satan is condemned to practise; all his acts are only actions, transient and ephemeral. The work of angels abides in eternity, because it is directed towards God and partakes in divine creativity. 'Bless the Lord, all his hosts, his ministers that do his will [*poiountes ta thelmata autou*]' (Ps. 103:20; Greek from LXX).

Unclean spirits in the New Testament

After the parable of Satan's scattered spoils, Jesus continues with a picture of the unclean spirit or demon having 'gone out of a man', wandering in desert places, 'seeking rest and finding none' (Luke 11:24). It may return, singly or with others, or enter the bodies of other living creatures, such as the Gadarene swine. Possession by evil spirits is a mysterious and complex idea, holding sway in many non-Christian religions. Such cults and folk traditions underlie many of the assumptions of the New Testament writers with regard to demons and unclean spirits. Through all ages, in ways too numerous to contemplate, the multiplicity of human ills has been assigned to spirits of evil, but the most important thing to remember is that evil spirits are totally overpowered by the love of Christ which is present in all love. This was Coleridge's meaning at the centre of the story told by his ancient mariner who is held under a curse, symbolized by the death of the albatross. Suddenly delighted with some water-snakes, the mariner says:

> A spring of love gushed from my heart
> And I blessed them unaware . . .
> The selfsame moment I could pray
> And from my neck so free
> The Albatross fell off, and sank
> Like lead into the sea.[4]

In the synoptic Gospels there are many references to the casting out of devils and unclean spirits by Jesus. Most of these references can be taken as the customary way of explaining diseases and their healing at that time. Jesus himself, as a man of his time, used these expressions in a general way. They should be included with his miracles of healing, and seen in the same light, which is always to place the emphasis first upon the faith of the person asking for healing; their faith will lead them to the gift of salvation. (The word 'salvation' is derived from the Latin for 'good health', 'well-being'.) In the episode of the boy whom we should now call epileptic, Jesus demonstrates plainly, even with impatience, that unless the sick are brought to him in faith there can be no miracle. The key to the story is in the need for faith rather than in defeating an unclean spirit. Only at Christ's feet is true healing found; the disciples had perhaps been trying to be clever (Mark 9:14f.).

Sickness is one of the great mysteries of suffering humanity; we shall never fathom it. The Gospel of John speaks very little of healing and not at all of unclean spirits; he always explains most carefully that the miracles were signs. The healing miracles are part of the work of Jesus on earth, revealing the love of God.

God anointed Jesus of Nazareth with the Holy Spirit and with power; he went about doing good and healing all who were oppressed by the devil, for God was with him (Acts 10:38).

Principalities and powers

The writers of the New Testament epistles speak frequently of 'principalities, powers, dominions' (in Greek *archēs, dunameōs, kyriotētos*) etc., titles which were used by Dionysius in his *Celestial Hierarchies*. They are cited by Paul and his followers chiefly to reiterate the meaning of the above statement from Acts. God in Jesus Christ is

Far above all principality, and power, and might, and dominion, [*archēs kai exousias kai dunameōs kai kyriotétos*] and every name that is named, not only in this world, but also in that which is to come (Eph. 1:21, AV)

'for God was with him' (Acts 10:38). The Epistle writers were more concerned to spread knowledge of the power of Christ, than that of angelic powers. Their use of this terminology is loose and inconsistent, and has to be read as the expression of background traditions, from Hebrew scriptures, Babylonian and Assyrian demonology, and Hellenistic deities, which formed the religious experience of many early Christian converts. In the New Testament names such as 'principalities' and 'virtues' have no specific reference; they are applied there generally to cosmic elemental powers, which were believed to be at work in human lives and in the fabric of the universe, influencing its course for evil more than for good (Eph. 6:12). Many such references in the Epistles are ambiguous: Otto Cullmann, in his book *Christ and Time*, writes that both the invisible 'princes' and their human instruments were included by Paul when he wrote: 'the wisdom of this age and the rulers of this age are doomed to pass away' (1 Cor. 2:6). Cullmann holds that the 'princes' of evil worked through human agents, i.e. Herod and Pilate, in the crucifixion of Christ. As we have suggested, Satan is confined to time and this world in all his works. The angels who fell in primeval time, says Cullmann, because they can only work in historical time, actually become part of the history of salvation.[5] The Devil was at work in the events of Jesus' death, as the Gospels say, but when it came to the resurrection Satan was powerless.

The *Catechism of the Catholic Church* also states that Satan's action is limited:

He cannot prevent the building up of God's reign. Although Satan may act in the world out of hatred for God and his kingdom in Christ Jesus, and although his action may cause grave injuries – of a spiritual nature and, indirectly, even of a physical nature – to each man and to society, the action is permitted by divine providence which with strength and gentleness guides human and cosmic history.[6]

The Catechism includes 'cosmic history' in this statement; the 'grave injuries' are probably intended to include the results of natural disasters as well as other evils, affecting people both individually and in large numbers. It is not always possible for us to discern the causes of various disasters in the world; sometimes they are evidently due to human sin, sometimes to natural hazards. In Hellenistic thinking the 'powers of the air' also influenced the forces of nature. The vision was coloured by concepts of humanity at the mercy of a hostile environment controlled by astral forces or intelligences. But nowadays we see the dangers encountered in the world by all creatures as integral to the design of the universe and its precarious structure. We have no way of knowing whether evil spirits are able to act directly upon the physical universe; the Catechism suggests that this is not so, but that their action is more likely to be purely 'spiritual'. While we no longer see the angels as in control of, say, the planets and stars, I think it is beyond us to define the scope for action of either good or evil spirits in the world. Perhaps the concepts of order and disorder as I have been discussing them can offer one way of looking at the question.

Faith in eternal life

I have defined order as proper relation, and suggested that the angels of God maintain their own relation to God in the whole 'order' of creation. Their task could be to keep every smallest part of the changing universe on course as it were, as creation passes into final perfection in God (cf. Romans 8:21). We cannot possibly conceive of order on such a large scale, and scientists continually present new theories of how the universe may be constructed and in what ways it changes through time. We should remember the promise of Christ that 'heaven and earth will pass away, but my words will not pass away' (Matt. 24:35). The apocalyptic visions in the Bible, which I shall discuss in the final part of this book, reveal angels at work in bringing about the final triumph of God over all evil. The universe and all it contains will be brought through evil into ultimate good. This is the 'order' that the angels are keeping. Satan's disordered angelic nature, on the other hand, could be set on introducing disorder, or evil, wherever possible, in vain attempts to slow down or pervert the progress of God's purpose. But because the Devil is confined to what is passing away, he has no possibility of destroying the words of Christ, who has 'the words of eternal life' (John 6:68).

Satan and his evil spirits can, however, use human weakness to create disorder; they are the blowflies of the angelic world, feeding on the corruption and decay of our mortal nature in its potential for evil. But the mortality of the material world is part of its ongoing life, so that decay and apparent disaster in the universe are not necessarily evil. People are capable of inflicting evil upon it, out of their own capacity to make disorder – to turn away from, or deny, their own higher potential, for example – and through the temptations of the evil spirits, who work upon us constantly. One of the ways they work is by persuading people to despair. Faith in God as holding the universe in his eternal love encourages hope, even in the face of the greatest human misery. At the heart of the Christian faith is acceptance of the cross and resurrection as one event. We cannot have Easter Sunday without the Friday and Saturday. Suffering is built into human existence, but every grief has the potential to pass into ultimate life. Pain is endured by the whole human race in solidarity, and in that there can be a flame of resurrection hope. Søren Kierkegaard said that despair is the 'sickness unto death'[7] (John 11:4).

Eventually the opposition of the Devil shall come to nothing, and some theologians hold that every spirit, good and evil, shall be gathered back into the complete and final design of creation, for all that God has made is good and redeemable. This belief queries the 'eternal' damnation of the Devil and all evil angels, in the 'place' (called Hell) assigned to them. Many people find it hard to accept that there can remain, in eternity, any spirit or soul away from God. The truth is beyond our understanding, while we are limited by language which can only form finite concepts, and the interpretation of texts is always open to question. In Acts Peter is quoted as referring to the 'time of restitution [*apokatastason*] of all things' (3:21, AV). Such a time could be the total recall and bringing together again of every part of creation into the merciful love of God. Even now, the fallen angels, having been created in that love, are essentially God's subjects still, so that their hostility is compelled to serve the final purpose for the world in Christ. In the cross the love of God is offered through the very event that appears to manifest the power of evil. But it was there that Christ opened his arms to embrace evil, to its uttermost. In his apparent abandonment to evil Jesus was closest to God and to the world. Whether or not we believe in Satan and his host, the Christian affirmation is that our closeness to God in Christ is unaffected by the worst evils that could meet us.

> For I am sure that neither death, nor life, nor angels, nor principalities, nor things present, nor things to come, nor powers, nor height, nor depth, nor anything else in all creation, will be able to separate us from the love of God in Christ Jesus our Lord. (Rom. 8:38)

Notes for Part I Chapter 5

[1] *The New Jerome Biblical Commentary* (Chapman, London, 1989) p. 239.
[2] F. Dostoevsky, *The Brothers Karamazov*, trans. Constance Garnett (Dent, London and Toronto; Dutton, New York, 1941).
[3] H. Alford, *The Greek Testament*, Vol. I (J. Rivington, London; J. Deighton, Cambridge, 1849) p. 513.

[4] S. T. Coleridge, 'The Ancient Mariner', lines 284–91.
[5] O. Cullmann, *Christ and Time*, trans. F. V. Filson (London, 1951) p. 191.
[6] Para. 325.
[7] S. Kierkegaard, *The Sickness unto Death*, trans. Walter Lowrie (Doubleday, New York, 1941).

PART II

Messengers

'I was sent to bring you this good news.'
(Luke 1:19)

1. By the Message of an Angel

The angel of the Lord declared to Mary.
And she conceived by the Holy Spirit.
(THE ANGELUS)

In the first part of this book the angels of God have been seen as mediatory creatures, who operate between the material and immaterial, and across the borders of the human and divine, and who, in bringing these together, reveal both the transcendence and the immanence of God. The second part sees them at work in history, where they have quite particular functions; the Bible shows them engaged in the redeeming of time. An angel messenger is a 'token of the word unheard, unspoken' which the angel is sent to speak, announcing events that lead to time's end, in God, and calling people to serve God in various ways.

Hebrew and Greek are alike in using the word for 'messenger' as the general title of spiritual beings in God's service. In both languages the word is used for any messenger. The Hebrew *'malakh'* frequently appears in the Bible to refer also to a human messenger. The Greek *'angelos'* was borrowed for the Latin Bible: Latin *'angelus'* has passed into other European languages to mean 'angel' exclusively. So the common designation of angels is the name of a function; they are performers, in living action. As messengers their action is proclaiming the word of God.

The word 'herald' may also be used to translate Greek *'angelos'*. The ceremonial office of a herald is a good analogy; he is one who carries and announces the message of another, especially of a prince or sovereign power; he announces the approach of another, he is a precursor; he makes royal proclamations on ritual occasions. A herald may be dressed in formal livery which distinguishes his allegiance, but his voice is his vehicle of expression; he himself is completely subjected to his role, to the words he proclaims. His very person is sacrosanct. For example, in the *Iliad*, Achilles greets the hostile envoys of Agamemnon with reverence: 'Hail, heralds, messengers of Zeus and men, draw near . . .'[1] Greek heralds had special duties at games and religious ceremonies; they were gifted with swift movement and clarity of voice. When, however, a herald becomes a messenger he may have more freedom in the execution of his duties. Whereas the herald simply gives out his proclamation, the messenger has a power of communication. By actually representing the sender of the message, the messenger enters into a relationship with the recipient. He can have a conversation, explain his mission, answer questions. Angels fulfil both functions; on occasions they appear as simple heralds, on others as messengers with freedom of response to the reactions of those to whom they are sent.

In the Old Testament, particularly in the earlier books, the *malakh Yahweh*, the angel of the Lord, very often utters words that come directly from the mouth of God; he is the voice of God. There have been various attempts to explain alternation in the text between God's immediate voice and the voice of his angel speaking for him. Some say we should understand that God's own voice is heard silently in the heart of the hearer, whereas the voice of an angel is heard as an external sound. Others that later editors tempered the daring notion that God spoke directly with Abraham, Moses, and others, by introducing the *malakh Yahweh* here and there to serve belief in the strict transcendence of God; when the narrative brings God into human perception, God must be represented by an angel; but this theory does not apply consistently. In whatever way one understands the purpose of the authors, the texts that introduce an angel as speaking for God describe the transmission of a message from God to someone on earth. That an angel, a spiritual messenger, should be given this task signifies the need for a mediator in such instances. The message itself is the movement from God to the human person.

Bearers of good news

Another Hebrew word for messenger is *mebasser*, which means 'the one bringing good news'. This word, like its equivalent in other Semitic languages, contains the sense of *good* news, joy and triumph. It is used particularly for a runner carrying home the news of victory in battle. The Greek verb *evangelizomai* likewise means 'to proclaim good news'; from it comes the New Testament *evangel*, 'the good news' of Christ. *'Mebasser'* occurs in Isaiah in a line that was borrowed from the writings of the prophet Nahum: 'How beautiful upon the mountains are the feet of *him who brings good tidings*, who publishes peace, who brings good tidings of good, who publishes salvation, who says to Zion, "Your God reigns"' (Isa. 52:7, my emphasis). In the preceding verse the voice of God is speaking: 'Therefore my people shall know my name; therefore in that day they shall know that it is I who speak; here am I' (Isa. 52:6). 'How beautiful on the mountains . . .' The runner, who races over the mountains bringing good news of salvation to the captive people of Jerusalem, is the word of God. He is beautiful (or 'seemly', 'fitting', 'seasonal') for that reason. The herald bringing news from battle was identified with his message, and treated accordingly. The role of messenger may thus incur danger. The herald takes risks, both in traversing the land, and in exposing himself as a personification of his message.[2] In the same way the messenger of God must be seen as an exposition of God's presence and power. 'Get you up to a high mountain, O herald of good tidings . . . say to the cities of Judah, "Behold your God!"' (Isa. 40:9)

'How beautiful upon the mountains are the feet of him who brings good tidings' became a favourite quotation in Jewish Rabbinical writings. It occurred frequently in their Messianic teaching, the promise of future peace. It was borrowed by Paul, who quoted it, with some alteration, in his letter to the Christians in Rome. Paul's rendering is significant, revealing that he was aware of the context of the quotation. He makes the messenger plural; for him they are the apostles and preachers of Christianity. Since all people are called to believe and be saved, their call must come through hearing about Christ. 'And how can men preach unless they are sent? As it is written "How beautiful are the feet of those who preach good news!"' (Rom. 10:14–15). The words from Isaiah serve not only as a lyrical embellishment. The approval and authorization of Scripture ratifies Paul's claim for the necessity of evangelizing all people; true apostles have a gracious task. But it is more than a matter of hearing, he goes on, for many have heard and not believed. If the word of Christ is heard, then faith will follow (cf. vv. 16 and 17). Paul is saying that in true apostles Christ himself is heard and seen. Jesus said to his apostles; 'He who hears you hears me, and he who rejects you rejects me, and he who rejects me rejects the one who sent me' (Luke 10:16). Paul has retained the kernel of Isaiah's message, indeed its fulfilment, and has brought out the New Testament understanding of *evangelizomai*. Christ himself is the content of the message, the good news of salvation and peace. His apostles, 'those who are sent', are his messengers. They serve, then, like angels.

Twice, in Acts, Luke tells how angels delivered messages of instruction to the evangelists. Philip the deacon left Peter and John after they had all returned to Jerusalem, being told by an angel to set off down the desert road towards Gaza. Philip soon came across an Ethiopian eunuch puzzling over the book of Isaiah. Philip taught him the fulfilment of Isaiah's prophecy, in Jesus Christ, and the eunuch was baptized by Philip, in a roadside pool (Acts 8:26–38).

> When they came up out of the water, the Spirit of the Lord caught up Philip; and the eunuch saw him no more, and went on his way rejoicing. But Philip was found at Azotus, and passing on he preached the gospel to all the towns till he came to Caesarea. (Acts 8:39–40)

Angels intervened in the conversion of another non-Jew, the centurion Cornelius (Acts 10). He and his household in

Caesarea had already turned away from the Roman gods, and were praying for further enlightenment. An angel 'in bright apparel' appeared to Cornelius as he prayed, addressing him by name. Cornelius, terrified, replied. 'What is it, Lord?' The angel told Cornelius that his prayers and alms had 'ascended as a memorial before God.' Cornelius was instructed to send to Joppa for Peter, so he dispatched two of his servants and a soldier to Joppa, having told them the whole story. (A reminder of the centurion who said to Jesus, 'When I say, go, they go.') Like angels, they were sent with a message for Peter; Peter, meanwhile, had also received a visionary message, which prepared him for the centurion's request. Peter was being taught, at the same time, how he must leave behind so much of the Jewish law and its prohibitions. Three times he was shown a 'sheet' filled with all kinds of animals, and an angel commanded him to kill and eat.

> But Peter said, 'No, Lord, for I have never eaten anything common or unclean.' And the voice came again, 'What God has cleansed you must not call common.' (10:14–15)

Peter did not at once understand the vision. It was only when the human messengers arrived that the angel gave him the clue:

> 'Behold, three men are looking for you. Rise and go down and accompany them without hesitation, for I have sent them.' (vv. 19–20)

Cornelius' men are surrogate angels. Peter went down at once, and said to the men, apparently before they spoke at all, 'I am the one you are looking for. What is the reason for your coming?' When he heard of the angel's visit to Cornelius, he invited the men into the house, and the next day they all returned to Caesarea. Peter had understood that 'God shows no partiality,' as he said to Cornelius, 'but in every nation anyone who fears him and does what is right is acceptable to him' (vv. 34–5). This was a very great lesson for Peter to learn; the strange vision and its spoken interpretation, repeated three times, were to shake him, to strike at his very roots, which had been in Judaism from birth. Cornelius, too, had a great conversion, but Peter's at this moment was perhaps greater. The Holy Spirit came, as at a second Pentecost, when Peter had revealed the gospel of Christ to the Roman household, and he authorized Christian baptism for them all.

Human messengers, breathing out, speak the words that have been given to them. They are an image of the spiritual messenger who actually is the breath of its message; the message can be seen as an inseparable part of its being. Not only is the command of God activated in the delivery of the message, but the words themselves bear divine power and are carried out in the action of the angel. 'So shall my word be that goes forth from my mouth; it shall not return to me empty, but it shall accomplish that which I purpose, and prosper in the thing for which I sent it' (Isa. 55:11). God sent his Son into the world; Christ is both the messenger and Word (just as he is both the door and the shepherd going through it). He is the perfect example of the angel-messenger who speaks always with God's voice. Jesus said, 'The word you hear is not mine, but the Father's who sent me.' 'He who speaks on his own authority seeks his own glory, but he who seeks the glory of him who sent him is true, and in him there is no falsehood' (John 14:24 and 7:18).

In the role of messengers, angels have no glory of their own, all their glory is the glory of God. The angel who speaks to John on Patmos, in John's Revelation, says, 'These are true words of God.' When John falls down at the angel's feet to worship, the angel says, 'You must not do that . . . worship God' (Rev. 19:9–10 and 22:8). If God creates angels to be his messengers, then their very existence is in God's word. Christ is the Word of God, so it is through Christ, not just by his example, that they speak. If he is the Word they speak, they will not deviate from their true message. The words of the message, spoken as it were by the expulsion of air from

God's mouth, are the angel's power and motivation, without which, we could say, the angel would not be. The Holy Spirit is its power, and its message. The effect of an angel's message is evidence of the 'breath' of the Spirit. The air of the world's atmosphere cannot be a wind unless it is moved, and the wind is not perceived except by its effects. Angel messengers can be understood as one kind of perceptible movement of the Holy Spirit. 'The wind blows where it wills, and you hear the sound of it, but you do not know whence it comes or whither it goes' (John 3:8); by analogy the angels are audible and visible movements of the Holy Spirit. And the angels themselves are spirit, the invisible creation; the metaphor may again be used to describe angelic action on the visible creation: the angel-spirit, or wind, blows among 'trees', 'leaves and branches' move.

Gabriel's annunciation to Mary

R. M. Rilke, the German poet, in one of his poems on the Annunciation, makes Gabriel say to Mary: *'Ich bin ein Hauch im Haim, du aber bist der Baum'* (I am the breeze within the wood, but you are the tree).[3] If there is nothing standing in the path of the wind, the wind has no effect; Gabriel's effectiveness was contingent upon Mary. He could have no word, could present no vision perhaps, at that moment, were it not for her for whom the message was intended. She could not respond until she experienced his arrival, the spirit's word, that would bring the arrival of the Spirit and the Word within her. Unique to Mary is the tacit implication in the text of the necessity for her compliance with the will of God. Another poet, W. H. Auden, wrote:

> To-day the unknown seeks the known.
> What I am willed to ask, your own
> Will has to answer; child, it lies
> Within your power of choosing to
> Conceive the child who chooses you.[4]

The moment of the incarnation of the Son of God was the moment when Mary said, 'Let it be to me according to your word' (Luke 1:38). Mary's words echo the creating word of God in Genesis: 'Let there be light [*Fiat lux*]', and so on. The word of the angel became the effective word of God; 'The Holy Spirit will come upon you . . .' (Luke 1:35); 'And God's spirit hovered over the water' (Gen. 1:2, JB). The dialogue between Gabriel and Mary ceased at once upon her '*Fiat*'; there was no more for the angel to do or say; he simply departed from her. Our interpretations can only be read off the surface of the scene, the written description of this real encounter. It was an encounter of such tension and life that out of it came the greatest action of the Holy Spirit.

In the Bible there are four separate scenes where a birth is predicted by the proclamation of an angel: two in the first chapter of Luke's Gospel, where Gabriel appears first to Zechariah and then to Mary; in Genesis 18 the birth of Isaac is finally promised when Abraham and Sarah are visited by three angelic beings; and in Judges 13 Samson's forthcoming birth is announced to his mother and her husband, Manoah. Gabriel's annunciation to Mary is the crown of all these texts. While it contains allusions to the other three scenes, the style of narrative is completely different. There is no descriptive detail; nothing detracts from the face-to-face meeting of Gabriel and Mary. Everything is in the simple exchange of words and the presence of one to the other. Concentration is total. No precise location is given; Mary could have been anywhere around Nazareth when Gabriel came and greeted her. It would be superfluous to describe a place: she herself is the holy ground. No actual vision is recorded. Nothing in the text tells us that Mary saw Gabriel, but it would be mistaken to take this omission for a definite statement. When Jacob wrestles with the angel there is no vision, but complete engagement. Mary's encounter with Gabriel must have involved her in no lesser way. Such reciprocation deploys the whole person; all the senses as well as the faculties of the mind are brought into operation.[5]

Mary was not called by the angel, as Moses is called by

name from the flaming centre of the bush, or Samuel in the temple. Was she perhaps ready for him? It is difficult, otherwise, to reconcile the delivery of such tremendous news with the idea of its young recipient being totally unprepared for it. The answer includes what the Church has long taught: Mary was prepared; she was conceived to be the Mother of God. We believe she was made ready by God, body and soul, to be a fit dwelling-place for the Son.[6] But the doctrinal answer does in itself explain her preparedness, if such she had, for this meeting with Gabriel. We could imagine for Mary a period of growing inner awareness that she was destined to fulfil a divine purpose. She would at first have dismissed such intimations as out of place, but was repeatedly brought back to them. They would have become clearer and more insistent until they were foremost in her thoughts and prayers, demanding answers; answers from God to her puzzlement, and an answer of acceptance from her. She may have learned more precisely that she was to conceive a child, and without any union with Joseph. The Gospel writer provides a hint that she confided in her cousin Elizabeth. Elizabeth's greeting of Mary included the words: 'Blessed is she who believed that there would be a fulfilment of what was spoken to her from the Lord' (Luke 1:45). Elizabeth could have been referring to the Messianic promise, but her words fit well with the possibility of a period during which Mary's faith and trust were tested.

Mary was certainly waiting; she may have been simply open to God in prayer and expectancy, the expectancy of all Jews (cf. Luke 2:38: 'Anna gave thanks to God, and spoke of him to all those who were looking for the redemption of Jerusalem'), but also an inner expectancy that God's plan would directly involve her, and demand her very self. When Gabriel arrived she knew at once that this was the fulfilment. The certainty was both terrifying and assuring; a complete falling into place of the long known, which she had not dared to acknowledge but had been insistently drawn to consider. Perhaps the voice was not new to her; Gabriel could have been speaking to her, progressively bringing the message into her consciousness. This arrival, however, was altogether different, and his greeting surprised her. It indicated the completeness of her favour with God. With it came the fear inherent in a fresh grasp of true knowledge. Gabriel gently confirmed her thoughts: Do not be afraid, Mary, for you *have* found favour with God, and behold, you *will* conceive . . .

Gabriel's message to Mary represents the Trinity, in its form of words: 'The Holy Spirit will come upon you, and the power of the most high [Father] will overshadow you; therefore the one to be born will be called holy, the son of God' (Luke 1:35). Gabriel speaks the action of the Triune God. His greeting to Mary named her as 'having been favoured' by God; she is now brought right into the life of the Holy Trinity, for she is integral to all three parts of Gabriel's proclamation. Her relation to the three Persons of God brought about the events that save the human race. Gabriel's relation to the Trinity, as he delivers his message, is the power through which those events were begun. Here we are presented with an aspect of the paradox of created free will: Gabriel depended upon Mary's freely given consent for his very being, for the possibility of his own free consent to carry out the will of God the Father, through the Son, in the Holy Spirit.

Gabriel, angel of the terrible holy countenance, has a simple demeanour before Mary. In the other annunciation scenes the angels, including Gabriel, appear lordly and majestic. Abraham prostrates himself, and runs to and fro to serve his visitors. In the temple with Zechariah Gabriel asserts his authority. At Nazareth the great angel waits on Mary, taking a subordinate position. She is afraid; her humility prevents her from realizing that the angel's whole manner is deferential to her. She does not ask for a sign. In fact she herself is the sign. This is subtly conveyed in the text through her question containing the statement that she is a virgin, which alludes to the prophecy of Isaiah: 'The Lord himself will give you a sign . . .' (Isa. 7:14); 'Behold a virgin shall conceive and bear a son, and his name shall be called Emmanuel' (Matt. 1:23). Isaiah's prophecy is used openly in Matthew's Gospel, as a gloss on the words spoken to Joseph by an angel. Joseph receives the message in a dream. His unquestioning obedience is proof of the power and immediacy of the experience, as well as of his own humility and openness to God.

The same can be said of the shepherds on the hillside near Bethlehem, who received the message of Christ's birth. The scene is so familiar that it is easy to reduce its dramatic nature, passing over it as merely another part of the Christmas decorations. But the 'glory of the Lord' in his angel appeared on that hillside, no less than in the chariots of fire above Dothan or the angels of God ascending and descending in Jacob's vision. It is consistent to assert that Gabriel was the angel who announced the nativity of the Saviour of the world, setting the seal on his particular commission. He was joined by a great number of angels whose song has been taken into the liturgy of the Church; or rather, the Church has joined her praise with that of the angels, in the words of their hymn.

The shepherds immediately went 'with haste' to find the child, an echo of Abraham's haste, under the terebinths of Mamre in Genesis 18. By contrast, when Gabriel appeared to Mary, their conversation has a quiet dignity which sets it far above the other annunciation exchanges. The writer of the cycle of mystery plays performed in Coventry in the Middle Ages evidently wished the action to move slowly, with pauses. He included this stage direction: 'Here the aungel makyth a lytyl restynge, and Mary beholdyth him.'[7] In Luke the only echo of Abraham's haste comes after Gabriel has departed from Mary, and she goes 'with haste into the hill country' to the house of Elizabeth (1:39).

Throughout the text of Gabriel's visit to Mary Elizabeth's pregnancy has formed a kind of peg, pinning the otherwise ethereal setting to the earth; it is the time-marker for the angel's appearance: 'In the sixth month . . .' (v. 26); it provides a direct allusion to Sarah, the mother of the Jewish nation: 'in her old age, . . . her who was called barren . . .' (v. 36); and it moves Mary to go in charity to her cousin's side as soon as the angel leaves her.

Notes for Part II Chapter 1

1 *Iliad* 1, 333–5.
2 cf. 2 Sam. 4:10 and 18:19–22, where heralds carry news of the death of King David's opponents, thinking such to be good news, *bessorah*; but for David the deaths of Saul and Absalom are the opposite. Joab knows well how David will greet the news of Absalom's death, and is reluctant to allow one of his own men to be the bearer. He prefers that a foreigner should run with it, death-bearing as it is.
3 R. M. Rilke, *'Verkündigung: Die Worte des Engels'*, *Gesammelte Gedichte* (Israel, Frankfurt-am-Main, 1962) p. 165.
4 W. H. Auden, 'For the Time Being' II, iii, *Collected Longer Poems* (Faber and Faber, London, 1968) p. 146.
5 In a spontaneous description of an angelic visitation, a friend of mine remarked that she felt she could finger the stuff of its garment.
6 *'Omnipotens sempiterne Deus, qui Virginis Mariae corpus at animam ut dignam Filii tui habitaculum effici meretur, Spiritu Sancto co-operante, praeparasti . . .'* (*Salve Regina* prayer).
7 P. Happé, ed. *English Mystery Plays* (Harmondsworth, 1975) p. 217.

2. Isaac

And the Lord appeared to Abraham by the oaks of Mamre, as he sat
at the door of his tent in the heat of the day. He lifted up his eyes
and looked, and behold, three men stood in front of him. When he
saw them, he ran from the tent door to meet them, and bowed
himself to the earth, and said, 'My Lord . . .'

(GEN. 18:1–3)

The opening sentence of the eighteenth chapter of Genesis is
a prologue; the reader is supplied with information not yet
known to Abraham. 'And [this is how] God appeared to
Abraham . . .' Abraham is resting from the midday sun, when
he looks up to see three men. The word 'angel' does not
appear in the text, but we have been told that the visitors
represent God; as such they may be called angels. Abraham's
immediate response signifies the extraordinariness of the
visitors; he seems to know at once that they have come from
God. There are other, more prosaic explanations for his reaction, i.e., that it was unusual for anyone to be travelling in
the heat of noon, and that Abraham's bow and then his
address of 'My Lord' were merely directed at the most noble-
looking of the three. These explanations may be included in
an overall grasp of the writer's intentions; not set in opposition to the more mysterious meanings, but held in balance
with them. Abraham's response is within convention, but we
know this is not just a conventional scene. Abraham says:
'My Lord, if I have found favour in your sight, do not pass by
your servant.' The writer of Luke's Gospel has echoed this
sentence in Gabriel's greeting and his reassurance of Mary,
and in her final acceptance as the handmaid of God.
Abraham offers hospitality, in modest terms: 'Let a little
water be brought, and wash your feet, and rest yourselves
under the tree, while I fetch a morsel of bread, that you may

refresh yourselves,' he says, 'and after that you may pass on – since you have come to your servant' (vv. 4–5).

The three men simply stand. When Abraham first sees them they are standing in front of him. Their only action throughout the first eight verses of the chapter is to reply to Abraham, with one voice, 'Do as you have said.' (In Hebrew this is literally; 'thus do, according to that which is your word,' again echoed by Luke in Mary's words, but the Greek Septuagint is not phrased in this way.) The statuesque dignity of the men governs the scene. It is thrown into relief by Abraham's haste. He runs to and fro until all is ready, then stands beside them while they eat. His hurry indicates awareness that the visitation is important. Eventually they speak (again with one voice): 'They said to him, "Where is Sarah your wife?"' (v. 9). The question is the revelation Abraham has awaited.

I have surmised that Mary was gradually prepared for the annunciation of Christ's conception. If this was so, her experience is prefigured in Abraham's long waiting time; twenty-five years during which he receives, so Genesis tells, promises from God that he will have many descendents, i.e., at least one son. For ten years after the first intimation of this promise he fathers no children at all, though the prediction is repeated six times, with increasing solemnity. Eventually he has a son by his wife's maid, Hagar (ch. 16). For thirteen years Abraham imagines that this son, Ishmael, is to be the father of the innumerable descendents who will be given the land of Canaan. Then he hears from God that Ishmael is not the son of the covenant, but that Sarai, to be renamed Sarah, will have a son whose name should be Isaac (17:15–21). Abraham is bewildered and astonished, for Sarai has always been barren and is then ninety years old. The arrival of the three men, at once recognizable as superior beings, could be the moment of final clarity. The mysterious men know Sarah's name; their opening question refers to her. At last Abraham will receive, from God in the speech of his messengers, the final promise of a son.

Abraham answers, 'She is in the tent.' The messengers

reply: 'At the appointed time I will return to you in the spring, and Sarah your wife will have a son,' repeating some of the phrases Abraham had received from God before, when God told him his son would be born, and that he must be named Isaac (17:16, 19 and 21). Sarah, who is listening, is unaware of this earlier message. It is the first time she has heard the promise, and she laughs at the idea. The narrator states openly what Abraham already understands, but Sarah does not: 'The Lord said to Abraham . . .' (18:13). The Hebrew uses the tetragrammaton 'Yahweh', the sacred name for God, which is always read aloud as 'Adonai' by the Jews. 'Adonai' is the Hebrew for 'lord', 'master' or 'prince', and it is used in its own form, possibly with deliberate ambiguity, when Abraham first addresses the visitors. The messengers now say to Abraham, 'Why did Sarah laugh, and say "Shall I indeed bear a child, now that I am old?" Is anything too hard for the Lord [Yahweh]? At the appointed time I will return to you, in the spring, and Sarah shall have a son.' (vv. 13–14) The angel of God is speaking; Sarah now perceives this, and is afraid, so she denies her laughter. The angel's rebuke is tempered for the reader, and for Abraham, by the knowledge that there is a play on words with the name of Isaac which means 'he laughs' in Hebrew. Sarah will laugh again, with true joy, at the birth of Isaac, and will invite everyone to join in her laughter (see Gen. 21:6 and cf. Luke 1:58).

The angel of God appears to Abraham in the form of three men; what is there is the action of God, what is seen is three men, or angels. With hindsight Christians can see, in the three angels, an image of the reality of the Trinity. The narrative has them speaking together, with one voice. This collective discourse presents them as a stylized group; they are one, and speak as one, though three, prefiguring Trinitarian theology. Augustine said of this passage: 'Why should we not accept that here is visibly introduced, through visible creatures, the equality of Trinity, and indeed, in the three persons, one and the same substance?'[1] It is one of the many Old Testament texts where Christian theology recognizes

107

prophecy. Augustine wrote, earlier in the same book, 'The Trinity works indivisibly in each sending or appearance [of itself].'[2] Every angel in its every mission, it could be said, carries out the will of the Three-in-One. In Luke, Gabriel's words actualized the work of the Trinity upon Mary. The appearance of the three angels at Mamre is closely related to the appearance of Gabriel to Mary. The former unique expression of the Holy Trinity in his angels rightly stands beside the annunciation of the Son's incarnation. Abraham receives his visitors with spontaneous hospitality. His action corresponds with Mary's acceptance of the will of God spoken in Gabriel's words.

The beautiful ikons which depict the hospitality of Abraham open 'a window or gateway on to the Divine'.[3] The three angels are painted as symbols of the three Persons of the Trinity, particularly in the ikon by Andrei Rublev. Rublev does not intend us to imagine that this is what the angels actually looked like, but meditation on their visitation can lead into a deeper knowledge of the presence of God and his love, as we see the way God came to Abraham, demanding his response. Rublev's ikon is entitled 'The Hospitality of Abraham'; Abraham received God, and as we stand before the ikon we can receive its grace, the grace of the Holy Trinity. The three men who come to Abraham bring him the same grace; therefore Rublev's representation is one with the angelic visitation. We see in the ikon three men manifesting a relationship of love; what is there is the love they symbolize.

The story of Sodom

When the three have delivered their message to Abraham they move on, towards Sodom (Gen. 18:16f.). Abraham goes with them 'to set them on their way', extending his hospitality the extra mile. Then the mystery of the nature of the three deepens. I think there is an example here of a shift in narrative technique, found often in the Old Testament in various ways, evincing its obscure origins. 'So the men turned from there, and went towards Sodom, but Abraham still stood before the Lord' (v. 22). Abraham then pleads with God not to destroy Sodom if there are any righteous men in the city (vv. 23–33). The next chapter opens: 'The two angels came to Sodom in the evening' (19:1). The 'three men' who walked towards Sodom have become 'two angels' upon their arrival. A literal reading of the story as continuous would have the three set out, with Abraham, towards Sodom; while Abraham holds discourse with one, supposedly the leading angel representing 'the Lord', the other two go on down to Sodom with orders to destroy it (cf. 19:13). They are greeted by Lot, Abraham's nephew, with kindness and hospitality that save them from the evils of the city, and they then rescue Lot and his family from the ensuing destruction (19:1–23). If, on the other hand, chapter 19 is read as a separate story, the change from one angelic function to another is clear, showing the possibility of seeing angels primarily in the light of their functions which do not easily merge. The angels at Mamre have come to bring God's message to Abraham and Sarah. In Sodom the angels are not messengers so much as ministers. As such they are completely different characters from the group of three. The story of the rescue of Lot and the destruction of Sodom is a separate narrative from the annunciation to Abraham and Sarah, divided from it by Abraham's pleading discourse with God (18:22–33), and the angels in it are not, I suggest, the same angels. The linking passage in the narrative is not concerned with angels at all, but with Abraham and God directly. The men could be understood as looking towards Sodom, knowing its fate. (The Sodom story will be further discussed in Part III where the work of angels as ministers is considered.)

The story of the visit to Abraham of the three men who speak as one demonstrates how God sends suitable messengers to announce the great events that are to forward his purpose. The atmosphere of solemnity and consequence evoked in the scene at Mamre is a measure of its significance, and is not matched in the mayhem of Sodom. Rublev's ikon distils this significance for Christians, who see in it the timelessness of the Word spoken in time. At Mamre Abraham, the father of the Jewish people who would bring forth Christ the Son of God in time, is host to the eternal Father, Son and Holy Spirit speaking through his angel messengers as one.

Notes for Part II Chapter 2

1 *De Trinitate*, II, xi (my translation). If we were to take Augustine's words as an explanation of the nature of the *angels* seen by Abraham, then 'one and the same substance' could only mean that there was actually one angel, appearing as three men.
2 ibid. II, i.
3 T. Castle, *Gateway to the Trinity* (St Pauls, Slough, 1988) p. 18.

3. John the Baptist and Samson

And there appeared to Zechariah an angel of the Lord standing on the right side of the altar of incense. And Zechariah was troubled when he saw him and fear fell upon him. But the angel said to him, 'Do not be afraid, Zechariah, for your prayer is heard, and your wife Elizabeth will bear you a son and you shall call his name John.'

(LUKE 1:11–13)

Abraham and Mary were, perhaps, ready for the appearance of angels; Zechariah, on the other hand, was taken by surprise. He was in the temple at Jerusalem. A priest, described with Elizabeth as 'righteous before God, walking in all the commandments and ordinances of the Lord, blameless' (Luke 1:6), it had fallen to his lot that day to enter the inner temple to burn incense at the altar. The writer thus brings the figure of Zechariah ritualistically to the inmost sanctuary of Jewish devotion, backed by the prayers of the people outside, and the holy city where the temple stands. As he proceeded with the ancient liturgy suddenly the angel of the Lord appeared to him. The prophet Malachi had foretold this moment:

> Behold, I send my messenger and he shall prepare the way before me, and the Lord whom you seek will suddenly come to his temple; the messenger of the covenant in whom you delight; behold, he is coming, says the Lord of Hosts. (Malachi 3:1)

The first sentence of this verse is quoted by all three synoptic gospels with reference to John the Baptist. The author of the original prophecy took the name 'Malachi', Hebrew for 'my

111

messenger'. When Christ used the prophet's words, as reported in Matthew and Luke's Gospels, he spoke of John as a messenger, his own forerunner, a second Elijah, but 'more than a prophet' (Matt. 11:9–14; Luke 7:26). Indeed, John the Baptist is sometimes pictured and referred to as an angel, because of the verse from Malachi. Its Greek *angelon* and Latin *angelum* used in the liturgy will have originated the concept, which appears in ikons and illustrations. Some ikons present John standing centrally with two great wings spreading from his shoulders and other reminders of his life and message, such as an axe set into the root of a tree, and a chalice bearing his severed head. The wings clearly symbolize the whole function of John, the angel-messenger whom God has sent beforehand. He was a voice. He directed attention away from his own person to his message. He was Christ's herald. Sometimes called 'the angel of the desert', he can also symbolize an angel's awesome aspect, sweeping in from the outer spaces to confront ordinary people with the sight of real holiness. His severed head shows the lengths they will go to eradicate such a sight.

While John was the last of the prophets, he is indeed 'more than a prophet'. There are links between John and Samson; the parents of each of them were instructed to dedicate their sons as 'nazirs' from birth. As well as refraining from strong drink, the nazirite forswears the use of a razor and cutting the hair. The hair of his head is consecrated to God, and so becomes holy (see Num. 6:18). Samson is a folk figure whose giant-like strength resides in his uncut hair. The wild and shaggy appearance of John the Baptist in the iconography recalls the sacred strength of Samson. (There are parallels to be found in shaggy demi-gods such as satyrs, wodwos and the green man of medieval legend.) John was not a supernatural being, neither angel nor giant. His role of messenger is unmatched, however, by any other human being. His advent was prophesied by his prophet forerunners. He came in order to bear witness to Christ the true light (John 1:6–8). Like an angel he reflected the divine light, but he was fully mortal. He received his message directly from God (John 1:33), but his knowledge of it was at times limited and uncertain (cf. Matt. 11:3). So the tradition of John 'the angel' is not unfounded; he represents a true angelic function, with the strange majesty of angelic power.

Gabriel's annunciation to Zechariah

'Who can endure the day of his coming and who can stand when he appears?' wrote Malachi (3:2). However awesome Zechariah's duty in the sanctuary of God, however firmly he believed himself to be in the presence of the Lord of Hosts at his altar, the actualization of the mystery was terrifying. Gabriel's first words to Zechariah were, 'Do not be afraid.' They imply: Do not fear my presence, and do not fear anything else, because my presence assures you all is well. 'Your prayer is heard . . .' Zechariah might have been actually asking for a son, in his prayer at the altar, or simply carrying the permanent sorrow of their childlessness. Anyway, the angel's words would have brought remembrance of similar announcements made to Abraham and Sarah, and other great Jewish forefathers. The angel concluded: 'You shall call his name John.' (The Hebrew *Jehohanan*, from which 'John' is taken, means 'gift of Yahweh'.) 'And you will have joy and gladness, and many will rejoice at his birth' (Luke 1:14). This is another allusion to the birth of Isaac; the words used by the Gospel writer echo the laughter of Abraham and Sarah. The Greek word for 'gladness' or 'laughter' here is the one used in the Septuagint to translate the Hebrew *yitsak* (Isaac), 'he laughs'. Buried clues reinforce the authority of the narrative; this is not just the account of one appearance of an angel to an old man, but a deeply significant portion of the whole of God's plan of salvation. It is inextricably ravelled with the stories that go before and after.

'For he will be great before the Lord, and he shall drink no wine nor strong drink, and he will be filled with the Holy Spirit, even from his mother's womb' (v. 15). Zechariah was told that John, like Samson, was to be set apart for the work of God. Samson was to have been a deliverer of Israel. The connection with him implies a wider consequence than merely the answer to Zechariah and Elizabeth's personal prayer. The angel said 'Do not be afraid, for your prayer is heard'; the words referred also to his priestly prayer, the supplication of the people of Israel, for whom Zechariah was offering the evening sacrifice. Fear not, for God does not forget his covenant. Zechariah was to play a part in the promise of salvation, his son would 'turn many of the sons of Israel to the Lord their God, and he will go before the Lord in the spirit and power of Elijah, to turn the hearts of the fathers to the children' (vv. 16–17). Malachi had written:

> Behold, I will send you Elijah the prophet before the great and terrible day of the Lord comes. And he will turn the hearts of the fathers to their children, and the hearts of the children to their fathers. (Malachi 4:5–6)

Zechariah heard Gabriel continue: 'and the disobedient to the wisdom of the just, to make ready for the Lord a people prepared' (v. 17).

The angel finished speaking. Zechariah's response shows that he could only grasp the part of the message that most closely related to himself: there was to be a miraculous gift of a son, after the manner of the great patriarchs. If it was true, then a sign should be given. 'How shall I know this?' (Literally, 'according to what shall I know this?') he asked the angel. Gabriel's immediate reply is to offer himself as the sign: 'I am Gabriel, who stand in the presence of God' (v. 19). The declaration of Gabriel's name fits into the narrative like a jigsaw piece, suddenly clarifying the picture. The name means 'lordly, or mighty, man of God'. The only place in the Old Testament where it appears is in Daniel, the book which brings the climax of messianic prophecy. There are many allusions to Daniel in the story of Zechariah in Luke's Gospel. After Daniel has seen a strange vision he says:

I sought to understand it; and behold, there stood before me one having the appearance of a man. And I heard a voice . . . calling, 'Gabriel, make this man understand the vision.' So he came near where I stood; and when he came I was frightened and fell upon my face, but he said to me, 'Understand, O son of man, that the vision is for the time of the end.' (Dan. 8:15–17)

Later, after Daniel has been fasting, and praying for the Jewish nation, Gabriel returns.

While I was speaking in prayer, the man Gabriel, whom I had seen in the vision at the first, came to me in swift flight at the time of the evening sacrifice. He came and he said to me, 'O Daniel, I have now come out to give you wisdom and understanding.' (9:21–2)

Still later, Gabriel comes again:

Then he said to me, 'Fear not, Daniel, for from the first day that you set your mind to understand and humbled yourself before God, your words have been heard.' (10:12)

To Zechariah Gabriel proclaimed himself as the sign, sent from God. His status 'in the presence of God' established Zechariah too, in the presence of God by his vision. The connections with Daniel are part of the sign Gabriel presented, his message 'for the time of the end', the fulfilment of the covenant. Gabriel said, 'I was sent to speak to you, and to bring this good news': the *evangel*, for which the message was the preparation.

From Gabriel the reader of Luke learns that Zechariah had doubts about the words of the message, the word of God. 'Behold, you will be silent and unable to speak until the day these tidings come to pass, because you did not believe my words which will be fulfilled in their time' (v. 20). The silencing of Zechariah was the result of his disbelief; it was the reassuring sign he had desired, also a punishment. The spoken word would be withdrawn from him because he withdrew from the word spoken to him by God. There are indications that he probably became both deaf and dumb. 'When he came out he could not speak . . . he made signs to them and remained dumb' (v. 22). The last word is *kophos*, which is also used in the New Testament for 'deaf', as a parallel with *alalos*, 'not speaking' (see Mark 7:37 and 9:25; Matt. 11:5). Gabriel's 'You will be silent' could be saying 'You will be deaf, *and* unable to speak'. The notion is confirmed later in the story of Zechariah, at the naming of John: 'And they made signs to his father, inquiring what he would have him called' (Luke 1:62). If Zechariah had been able to hear there would have been no need to make signs to ask him a question.

When he emerged from the temple Zechariah had been changed, not only by his deaf-and-dumbness. 'They perceived that he had seen a vision in the temple' (v. 22). A parallel to this is the illuminated face of Moses after he has been speaking with God (Exod. 34:29–35). Zechariah, too, exhibits visible signs that he has been in the divine presence. After his time of silence the effect of his experience is further manifested in an articulate prophetic spirit (see Luke 1:67f.).

Angels in time and space

The final part of the angel's message included an accent on time as well as on speech and words. The angel was sent in time, and came with speech, itself a time-sequence of words. 'Time' was Gabriel's last word to Zechariah who would be silent until 'the day that these things come to pass; . . . my words which will be fulfilled in their time.' At this point in the narrative the scene changes from inside the temple to outside, and the angel's departure is not described. But there follows a subtle reminder of duration, of the angel's action in space and time: 'And the people were waiting for Zechariah, and they wondered at his delay in the temple.' Every angelic appearance brings together time and eternity, since angels exist outside time, yet they come into the temporal world, where they act in time. When an angel foretells a birth, time is of particular significance; the content of a message that a child will be born carries its own time-span of gestation. Twice the angel says to Abraham, 'I will return to you *at the time of life* [literal translation], and Sarah will have a son' (Gen. 18:10 and 14). The Hebrew phrase is mysterious, and has been variously interpreted: 'the spring time', 'a nine-month period', 'when the season comes', etc., but it is triumphantly summed up in Genesis 21:2: 'And Sarah conceived and bore Abraham a son in his old age at the time of which God had spoken to him.' The birth of the child will reveal the truth of the prediction, but the child is already present as it grows in the womb. All the annunciation scenes we are discussing bear this significance; each is a 'point of intersection of the timeless with time' symbolizing the *pleroma*, the 'fullness of time', in which the hour of the incarnation is united with the end of time, when Christ will return. His second coming will be the final revelation of his constant presence: 'Lo, I am with you always, to the close of the age' (Matt. 28:20). Gabriel's role as messenger of the incarnation enacts uniquely the mystery of eternity as ever-present in the now.

Samson

The birth of Samson was also predicted by angelic annunciation:

> There was a certain man of Zorah, of the tribe of the Danites, whose name was Manoah; and his wife was barren and had no children. And the angel of the Lord appeared to the woman and said to her, 'Behold, you are barren and have no children, but you shall conceive and bear a son.' (Judg. 13:2–3).

The visitation of an angel of God to the parents of Samson is an incident of the long years between the birth of Isaac and the birth of John the Baptist, the last prophet of the old dispensation. The fortunes of the children of Abraham, Isaac and Jacob ebb and flow dramatically. In the book of Judges we see them in the stormiest era of all; they are continually assailed by enemies, and continually turning away from God to go their own way in both worship and morals. The book covers an age of transition, between Moses and David. It is a liminal period, as the Israelites move on to borderlands, crossing various thresholds. They are now without the mediation of a great leader. Divine mediators appear; angels bring messages, predictions, and calls from God to his people.

In chapter 2 God's messenger traverses earthly boundaries: 'Now the angel of the Lord went up from Gilgal to Bochim' (Judg. 2:1). Gilgal was established as a holy place after the Israelites had crossed the Jordan into Canaan, and Joshua set up the twelve stones there, taken from the bed of the river when the people walked across dryshod (Josh. 4:19–24; see chapter 1, Part I above). This sanctuary signifies the deliverance of the twelve tribes conducted safely through the wilderness by angelic guidance. The angel now comes from Gilgal to an unknown place, where he speaks for God; 'I brought you up from Egypt, and brought you into the land which I swore to give to your fathers' (Judg. 2:1). He comes to pronounce divine judgement: after this the people will suffer under many different human judges. Because they have disobeyed God, their enemies will not be entirely vanquished, but will remain as adversaries and temptations to evil. 'When the angel of the Lord spoke these words to all the people of Israel, the people lifted up their voices and wept. And they called the name of that place Bochim ['weepers']; and they sacrificed there to the Lord' (vv. 4–5). This place also becomes sanctified, by a river of tears rather than the miraculously dry stones from Jordan. Moving between the two places the angel demonstrates a correlation between triumph and sorrow; both are offered in sacrifice.

God will give his people relief from time to time. Subsequent chapters of Judges tell of the overcoming of Israel's enemies periodically by chosen men and women: Othniel, a judge, receives the spirit of the Lord, and conquers the king of Mesopotamia; the Canaanites are defeated through the word of the prophet Deborah, together with the action of Jael, wife of a loyal wandering Israelite. The Midianites are overcome by Gideon, called by the angel of God to this task, and the Ammonites fall to Jephthah, another who receives the spirit of the Lord (Judg. 3;4;6;11). Samson, Manoah's son, is to 'begin to deliver Israel from the hand of the Philistines'. God sends his angel to announce that help is coming yet again. God will never desert his people; never will he deny his covenant. Angels are signs of his presence among them, walking with them through history. Each angelic appearance is part of the catena of such appearances continuing to the end of time.

Samson's birth announced

The angel of the Lord appeared to the woman and said to her, 'Behold, you are barren and have no children, but you shall conceive and bear a son. Therefore beware, and drink no wine or strong drink, and eat nothing unclean, for lo, you shall conceive and bear a son. No razor shall come upon his head, for the boy shall be a Nazirite to God from birth; and he shall begin to deliver Israel from the hand of the Philistines.' (Judg. 13:3–5)

The angel of Samson's birth appears first to his mother. (She shares with Mary the few appearances of angels to women in the Bible. The others are Hagar, and the women who spoke with the angels of Christ's resurrection, at the empty tomb.) The angel tells Manoah's wife that from birth her son shall be separated from ordinary children. He shall be a nazir, and in this case, unusually, the mother is instructed to refrain from strong drink. Manoah's wife goes to tell her husband of the message:

'A man of God came to me, and his countenance was like the countenance of the angel of God, very terrible; I did not ask him whence he was and he did not tell me his name; but he said to me, "Behold you shall conceive and bear a son; so then drink no wine or strong drink, and eat nothing unclean, for the boy shall be a Nazirite to God from birth to the day of his death."' (vv. 6–7)

The woman is confused. She dare not think of the man as more than a prophet, yet he had the aspect of superhuman holiness. The Hebrew *nora* is used for the terrible majesty of God himself (cf. Exodus 15:11). In repeating the message she adds a phrase of her own about the boy: 'to the day of his death'. She omits that his task will be to defend Israel from the Philistines; therefore Manoah is altogether mystified. He prays that the man may return:

'O Lord, I pray thee, let the man of God whom thou didst send come again to us, and teach us what we are to do with the boy that will be born.' (v. 8)

Manoah does not know he is asking to see an angel, but as such his prayer is unique in the Bible. Angels do not appear on demand, nor do people request to see them. However,

God listened to the voice of Manoah, and the angel of God came again to the woman as she sat in the field; but Manoah her husband was not with her. And the woman ran in haste and told her husband, 'Behold, the man who came to me the other day has appeared to me.' And Manoah arose and went after his wife, and came to the man and said to him, 'Are you the man who spoke to this woman?' And he said, 'I am.' And Manoah said, 'Now when your words come true, what is to be the boy's manner of life, and what is he to do?' (vv. 9–12)

Manoah displays the kind of trust that Joseph possessed to an even greater degree when he accepted the message about Mary given to him by the angel, in his dream. Manoah has prayed for the message from God to be made clearer. He expects the prophet to return and speak to him. However, the 'man of God' appears again to the woman. Manoah goes straight to him, to ask his question. Unlike Zechariah, Manoah does not doubt the effectiveness of the message; he asks the reason for the instructions. The angel's only answer is that the woman must do all that he has commanded her (v. 13).

> And Manoah said to the angel of the Lord, 'Pray let us detain you, and prepare a kid for you.' And the angel of the Lord said to Manoah, 'If you detain me, I will not eat of your food; but if you make ready a burnt offering, then offer it to the Lord.' (For Manoah did not know that he was an angel of the Lord.) (vv. 15–16)

After the manner of Abraham, Manoah offers hospitality to the visitor. The reply contains signs that Manoah entertains an angel but he continues to read them as from a holy man bound to asceticism and in the service of God. Manoah and his wife live at a holy place: Zorah has a sacred rock, or altar stone. The couple are familiar with the rituals and the significance of such places, which foreshadow the temple altar where Zechariah performed his duties. Zechariah was in the act of making an incense offering when Gabriel came to him. Manoah is told to prepare a holocaust, which will prove to be the revelation of the angel. Manoah would understand that the sanctification of his wife, himself and the child they are to conceive will be confirmed in this offering upon the sacred rock. It is all in keeping with the visit of a holy man of God, and shall be carried out with proper ceremony. Manoah's manner is deferential:

> And Manoah said to the angel of the Lord, 'What is your name, so that, when your words come true, we may honour you?' And the angel of the Lord said to him, 'Why do you ask my name, seeing it is wonderful?' (vv. 17–18)

The angel's reply begins with exactly the same words spoken to Jacob as he wrestled (Gen. 32:39). It is the code for 'I am not merely a man, with a man's name, do you not perceive this?' Jacob received a blessing. Manoah is blessed with the mysterious words 'It is wonderful'. (There is no qualifying conjunction in the Hebrew.) *Peli*, 'incomprehensible' or 'marvellous'[1] can indicate both that this is the name, or nature of the angel, and that it is impossible to give a name to a messenger from heaven. This 'name' appears again, in the next verse:

> So Manoah took the kid with the cereal offering, and offered it upon the rock to the Lord, to him who works wonders. (v. 19)

The translation of this verse presents difficulties. The Hebrew for the last five words is literally 'a wonder to work'. This has been applied to God, as in the translation above, but it really refers to God's action in the angel, as Manoah offers the kid for a whole offering, together with the requisite cereal offering (see Numbers 15).

> And when the flame went up toward heaven from the altar, the angel of the Lord ascended in the flame of the altar while Manoah and his wife looked on; and they fell on their faces to the ground. (v. 20)

At last God has truly manifested his presence in his angel, by the holy flame, in which the angel ascends, 'while Manoah and his wife looked on'. In the Hebrew that phrase occurs at the end of verse 19 and again here. Emphasis is laid on 'seeing'. The other three birth proclamations all concentrate on the dialogue, but in this episode the sight of the angel is important. Firstly his 'terrible' aspect, then the three successive appearances, and finally his ascent in the fire are all to leave a visual impression upon the couple that is unmistakeable:

> Then Manoah knew that he was the angel of the Lord, and Manoah said to his wife, 'We shall surely die, for we

have seen God.' But his wife said to him, 'If the Lord had meant to kill us, he would not have accepted a burnt offering and a cereal offering at our hands, or shown us all these things, or now announced to us such things as these.' (vv. 21–3)

It is the woman who sees the full significance of the angel's ascent in the flame. Their offering has been accepted by God, the sure sign that all they have experienced is true.

Notes for Part II Chapter 3

[1] cf. Isa. 9:6: 'His name shall be called Wonderful' (*peli*). 'Wonderful' should not be used as an adjective here, as in many translations; it is one of the list of names: 'Wonderful, Counsellor, Mighty God, Everlasting Father, Prince of Peace'. Handel's *Messiah* brings this across very well.

4. Gideon, Moses and Isaiah

Now the angel of the Lord came and sat under the oak at Ophrah,
which belonged to Joash the Abiezrite, as his son Gideon was
beating out wheat in the wine press, to hide it from the Midianites.
(JUDG. 6:11)

The story of Gideon begins in chapter 6 of the book of Judges.
To escape the ravaging hosts of Midian the Israelites have
taken to the hills. They are hiding in caves. 'And Israel was
brought very low because of Midian; and the people of Israel
cried for help to the Lord' (v. 6). A prophet is sent to them,
but he simply repeats the formula: 'Thus says the Lord, the
God of Israel; I led you up from Egypt . . . but you have not
given heed to my voice' (vv. 8, 10). In the next verse we see
the arrival of the *malakh Yahweh*, who will make things
happen. Christ spoke of John the Baptist as 'more than a
prophet'; John was more like an angel. Angels are more than
prophets, for their speech is always action, the action of the
Word of God. Manoah and his wife thought they were
speaking with a prophet, but discovered that their visitant
was more than a prophet; it was an angel they had seen, in
whom God manifests himself, and in whom his word is
carried out.

The scene of Gideon's call (which precedes the birth of
Samson) bears many similarities to the various birth
announcements, particularly that of Samson. It also runs
parallel to other 'calls'; i.e., to Moses, Jeremiah and Isaiah.
In a sense the call is to birth, the rebirth of the one called to
completely new life, of service to God. In this chapter of
Judges the prophet says, 'Thus says the Lord . . .' He is simply
repeating a message, like a herald. The divine messenger's
opening words to Gideon are, 'The Lord is with you,' meaning
both by the angel's presence, and in Gideon himself. God's

continuing presence with the person he calls is the only thing that makes acceptance of the call possible. By sending his angel to speak he guarantees this presence from the beginning. The new life will be a life in and with God, and God will always be with and in his servant.

Gideon is threshing wheat deep down in the pit of a winepress, to hide the grain from the Midianites. The reader of the narrative has first sight of the angel sitting under the oak at Ophrah nearby, but apparently unseen by Gideon. When he does see the angel, Gideon's ignominious position makes the angel's greeting seem ironic: 'The Lord is with you, you mighty man of valour' (v. 12). Gideon gives a sharp reply: 'Pray, sir, if the Lord is with us, why then has all this befallen us? And where are all his wonderful deeds which our fathers recounted to us saying, "Did not the Lord bring us up from Egypt?"' (v. 13). Gideon has evidently had enough of prophets; he does not yet know that this is more than a prophet.

And the Lord (*Yahweh*) turned to him and said, 'Go in this might of yours and deliver Israel from the hand of Midian; do not I send you?' (v. 14)

The response made by Gideon is in tune with those of Moses, Isaiah and Jeremiah, and all of us who feel inadequate to the demands made on us. 'Pray, Lord, how can I deliver Israel? Behold, my clan is the weakest in Manasseh, and I am the least in my family' (v. 15). He has not yet understood that it is God who has 'turned towards' him, and that his 'might' is not his own, but is bestowed on him by this divine messenger. The angel comes further into the open. 'But I will be with you, and you shall smite the Midianites as one man' (v. 16). Gideon's whole manner changes in the next verses which are the turning-point of the story. His discourse now takes on a reverent tone, brought out clearly by the translation in the Revised Standard Version of the Bible:

If now I have found favour with thee, then show me a sign that it is thou who speakest with me. Do not depart from here, I pray thee, until I come to thee, and bring out my present, and set it before thee.' (vv. 17–18)

Before this Gideon has addressed the man as *Adonai*, or 'Sir'; now he knows he is addressing God's representative. His request for a sign is both for the confirmation of this understanding, and that he may make concrete acknowledgement, by an offering for sacrifice. (The word translated as 'present' carries this meaning.) He knows that the *malakh Yahweh* may disappear at any moment. The angel replies 'I will stay till you return.' (v. 18)

Gideon brings out meat and cereal offerings. The angel instructs him to lay the sacrifice on the rock of Ophrah, under the oak. (This rock may have been a Canaanite altar.) The mystery of the angelic nature emerges here. While the angel 'is' God himself in his speech with Gideon, he is at the same time the servant of God, and he will always render worship and praise to his maker. So Gideon and the angel together offer the sacrifices to Almighty God. In our liturgy too, we join with the angels in their everlasting hymn of praise, and we ask that our offering may be acceptable to God with assistance of his angels. Since the fourth century or earlier the Church has prayed in the Eucharist 'that your angel may take this sacrifice to your altar in heaven . . .' (see chapter 4, Part III below). Gideon's sacrifice receives the sign of sacred fire, and the angel's ascent betokens its acceptance on the heavenly altar:

> The angel of the Lord reached out the tip of the staff that was in his hand, and touched the meat and the unleavened cakes; and there sprang up fire from the rock and consumed the flesh and the unleavened cakes; and the angel of the Lord vanished from his sight. (v. 21)

At the revelation Gideon is afraid. He turns at once to God in prayer, since he knows he has seen the terrible majesty of the angel of God. 'Alas, O Lord God! For now I have seen the angel of the Lord face to face!' But the Lord said to him,

'Peace be to you; do not fear, you shall not die.' (vv. 22–3) From then on Gideon is 'clothed' with the spirit of the Lord.[1] Before he begins his war upon the Baal-worshipping Midianites he consecrates the altar at Ophrah, now sanctified, calling it 'The Lord is Peace' (v. 24).

The call of Moses

Moses spoke with God 'face to face' and lived (Exod. 33:11), but first God called him through an angel, and again with the sign of fire.

> Moses was keeping the flock of his father-in-law Jethro, the priest of Midian; and he led his flock to the west side of the wilderness, and came to Horeb, the mountain of God. And the angel of the Lord appeared to him in a flame of fire out of the midst of the bush; and he looked, and lo, the bush was burning, yet it was not consumed. And Moses said, 'I will turn aside and see this great sight, why the bush is not burnt.' When the Lord saw that he turned aside to see, God called to him out of the bush, 'Moses, Moses,' and he said 'Here am I.' (Exod. 3:1–4)

The call of Moses (who precedes Gideon by several generations) begins, rather than ends, with fire. The fire in the bush symbolizes original fire, from which all fire is born. Sacred flames, like those in the stories of Manoah and Gideon, which burn sacrifices at the angels' command, come from this fire. It is fitting that this fire is itself an angel: 'He makes his angels winds and his ministers flaming fire' (Ps. 104.4).[2] The reader, however, has the privilege of being told that the fire is the *malakh Yahweh*; Moses himself only sees a strange sight, fire in the middle of a bush that does not burn away. Seeing comes first; Moses turns aside, to see, and his eyes are opened. After this he will see everything in a new way. The fire is fire of initiation, creation and sanctification. When Moses stops to look, God opens his ears also; his name is called, and then his mouth is opened in speech: 'Here am I' (Hebrew: *hineni*).

'God called to him . . .' God speaks through his angel who is made a flaming fire for the purpose of this encounter. A created voice utters God's call to Moses, and continues in dialogue with him. The 'voice of God' can represent the presence of God: Adam and Eve 'heard the voice of the Lord God walking in the garden in the cool of the day' (Gen. 3:8, AV). Once God has gathered Israel into a nation under Moses as lawgiver, the term becomes synonymous with the will of God for his people; e.g., 'You did not obey the voice of the Lord your God' (Deut. 28:62); and God says, 'If you will obey my voice and keep my covenant, you shall be my own possession among all peoples' (Exod. 19:5; see also Num. 14:22; Deut. 4:30, etc.). From the bush the voice of God is heard through the angel of fire.

'Do not come near; put off your shoes from your feet, for the place on which you are standing is holy ground' (Exod. 3:5). The ground is thrice holy; already walking upon the mountain of God, Moses comes to this particular spot where God has chosen to meet him, and the sacred fire is the visual sign of its sanctification by the angel of God. A subtle emphasis is contained in the Hebrew, which is impossible to translate. It might be, 'where you stand, earth-of-holiness it is.' The burning bush makes even the surrounding area sacred. God is present. There are numerous reasons for the tradition of removing shoes before treading on sacred ground. As well as being a sign of humility and respect, it ensures that contact with the ground is unimpeded (literally) and the ambient holy aura received freely and purely.[3] Moses hears the voice of God continue:

I [am] the God of your father, the God of Abraham, the God of Isaac, and the God of Jacob.

(There is no verb 'to be' in this sentence, a common grammatical construction in Hebrew.)

And Moses hid his face, for he was afraid to look at God. (v. 6)

Sight is now less important than hearing, but nevertheless the fire burns in the bush all through the encounter; Moses dare not look. We cannot separate the theophany into parts, as some commentators have done, saying that the call is in a different mode from the vision. The fire is central to the meeting of Moses with God in his angel.[4] The sacred flame must burn on until the dialogue comes to a close.

In the next three verses Moses hears that God is calling him to lead the Israelites out of their oppression in Egypt.

> But Moses said to God, 'Who am I that I should go to Pharaoh, and bring the sons of Israel out of Egypt?' He said, 'But I will be with you; and this shall be the sign for you, that I have sent you: when you have brought forth the people out of Egypt, you shall serve God upon this mountain.' (vv. 11–12)

These words are spoken out of the fire. The fire itself is the sign, which will be renewed in a great volcano of fire on the same mountain three months after the escape from Egypt. Then 'Mount Sinai [Horeb] was wrapped in smoke because the Lord descended upon it in fire' (Exod. 19:18). As Moses later reminded the people:

> Out of heaven he let you hear his voice, that he might discipline you; and on earth he let you see his great fire, and you heard his words out of the midst of the fire. (Deut. 4:36)

God again descends upon the mountain in fire when Moses is given the stone tablets inscribed with the law:

> Now the appearance of the glory of the Lord was like a devouring fire on the top of the mountain in the sight of the people of Israel. And Moses . . . went up on the mountain. And Moses was on the mountain forty days and forty nights. (Exod. 24:17–18)

There is a strong tradition that the law was given to Moses by the angels of God.[5] The angel of fire in the bush prefigures the flames of fire on Mount Sinai as the glory of God descends, and Moses receives the law, the law which will thenceforth be the 'voice of God'.

The sign of fire, given by the angels to Gideon and Samson's parents to consume their sacrifices, also has its meaning in these flames. Miraculous fire is the glory of God made visible, signifying God's very presence. Elijah, in his turn, calls down supernatural fire upon his sacrifice, to demonstrate the power of the one true God as against the nothingness of Baal (1 Kgs 18:36f.). (Mendelssohn, in his oratorio 'Elijah', has Elijah pray at this moment: 'O Thou, who makest thine angels spirits; thou whose ministers are flaming fires, let them now descend!') The angels of fire do descend upon the offering which, in spite of being saturated with water, burns at once.

After that episode Elijah escapes from Jezebel and the prophets of Baal, to spend forty days and nights travelling to Mount Sinai, where Moses had waited for the angels of fire to bring the law. Before his journey Elijah is strengthened with food provided by an angel. (1 Kgs 19:5–8; see chapter 3, Part III below.) On the mountain he experiences earthquakes, wind and fire. However, the Lord is not in the fire, though it is apparently a supernatural fire, burning nothing. God comes to Elijah in a whisper, a barely discernible voice in a tiny breeze. 'He has made his angels winds . . .' When Elijah hears it he hides his face, as Moses did (1 Kgs 19:11–13). A chain of signs is formed, beginning with the burning bush, continuing through the theophany on Sinai, to Elijah's encounter with God on the same mountain, and reaching their fulfilment in the transfiguration of Christ. Moses and Elijah were present together at that great theophany, 'on a high mountain', when Jesus revealed his divinity in the sight of Peter, James and John. The flames in the bush, the mighty fires and the awe-inspiring voice of God, are all preparations for the coming of Christ who is the only actual manifestation of God himself here on earth. The way is prepared for him by the angels and prophets: the angels as wind and fire, the prophets instructed by them, and by them sustained in the desert experience, which Christ also suffered.

> Then Moses said to God, 'If I come to the people of Israel and say to them, "The God of your fathers has sent me to you," and they ask me, "What is his name?" what shall I say to them?' God said to Moses, 'I am who I am.' And he said, 'Say this to the people of Israel, I am has sent me to you.' (Exod. 3:13–14)

Moses obliquely asks the name of God, which is far more than asking the name of the angel of God. In this unique moment in all God's dealings with humanity God gives himself a name in human language: *EHYEH ASHER EHYEH*, 'I am what I am', or 'I will be what I will be'; the Hebrew verb is in the causative mode, and our translations can only approximate to it. Converted to the third person, the verb becomes something like *YAHWEH*, 'He is'. Another way of hearing it might be: 'I am nothing other than what I am' – I am not this flame, nor this voice, nor these words. I am purely and simply what I am. God has, however, made his angels fire and winds to be his voice, so that we may hear the Divine pronouncement: I am.

The call of Isaiah

The call of Isaiah comes in chapter 6 of his book. It is not a call in the same sense that Moses and Gideon are called to a new life in the service of God. Isaiah is already a prophet, speaking his vision 'in the days of Uzziah' and continuing to speak during the reigns of subsequent kings. He is qualified to be God's instrument. The call in chapter 6 could be a justification of his pronouncements,[6] but the scene is on a higher plane than that of simply providing a warrant.

> [It was] in the year of the death of King Uzziah; and I saw the Lord seated upon a high throne, raised up, and the

skirts of his robe filled the inner temple. (v. 1, my translation)

This is an apocalyptic vision, of which I shall say more in the final part of this book. It also has a place here. Above and around the Almighty King stand angels; six-winged seraphs, who cry out, antiphonally, a hymn of praise to God:

'Holy, Holy, Holy is the Lord of Hosts; the whole earth is full of his glory.' And the foundations of the thresholds shook at the voice of him who cried, and the house was filled with smoke. (v. 3, RSV)

Isaiah hears an angel's voice. He experiences the heavenly liturgy as it is sung to perfection. At once his own voice seems to him less than worthless.

'Ah, woe is me, for I am silenced. [The Hebrew word carries the meaning "struck dumb" as well as "ruined" or "destroyed".] For I am a man of unclean lips, and I dwell in the midst of a people of unclean lips, and my eyes have seen the King, the Lord of Hosts!' (v. 5)

Isaiah fully realizes the danger in seeing across the bounds of the human into the divine. The very foundations of the thresholds are shaking. Before he can speak again he must be ritually purified. He is initiated by hearing the highest created voice, that of the angels around the throne of God, singing the greatest song of praise. Purgation by supernatural fire follows:

Then flew one of the seraphim to me, having in his hand a burning coal which he had taken with tongs from the altar. And he touched my mouth and said, 'Behold, this has touched your lips; your guilt is taken away, and your sin forgiven.' And I heard the voice of the Lord saying, 'Whom shall I send, and who will go for us?' Then I said, 'Here am I! Send me.' (vv. 6–8)

Isaiah's mouth, cleansed by the fire, is opened to give the proper response to God's call: *hineni*, 'Here am I'. It is the service of his mouth that God demands: 'And [God] said: "Go, and say ..."' (v. 9). Isaiah is to be a messenger, to speak 'the voice of God' to his people. He would not be able to undertake this task unless God had first called him, invited him over the threshold into his very presence. 'I will make him draw near, and he shall approach me, for who would dare of himself to approach me?' (Jer. 30:21)

The purging fiery coal has taken Isaiah into a higher way of prophecy, with relation to the angel messengers. These particular angels are given the title 'seraphim' which occurs nowhere else in the Bible. The word can mean 'burning ones', and it has been suggested that a personification of lightning could be intended.[7] The seraphim have been associated with fire through long Christian tradition, which also draws on more ancient notions whereby the highest angelic spirits inhabit the upper air, or empyrean (the sphere of fire). For our purpose they bear close relation to the angel of fire in the bush and to the fire of God's glory on Mount Sinai.

Fire of the Spirit

At the beginning of this book the angels made their entrance in the form of chariots of fire. Later I shall discuss Ezekiel's vision of the great fiery chariot. The perilous quality of fire carries a powerful significance. It is appropriate that a Rabbinical tradition declares great risk involved in meditating upon Ezekiel's first chapter. To do so is to play with fire.[8] An anecdote expresses this well:

> Once as Ben Azzai sat and expounded, the fire played round him. They went and told rabbi Akiba, saying, 'Sir, as Ben Azzai sits and expounds, the fire is flashing round him.' Rabbi Akiba went to him and said: 'I hear that as you were expounding, the fire flashed round you. Were you treating of the secrets of the Chariot?' 'No,' he replied, 'I was only linking up the words of the Torah with

one another and then with words of the prophets, and the prophets with the writings, and the words rejoiced as when they were delivered from Sinai, and they were sweet as at their original utterance.'[9]

Ben Azzai's reply offers a picture also of the chain of signs beginning with Moses and completed in Christ.

Fire is mysterious, even in its natural form, but supernatural fire defies any understanding since it can present opposing qualities, 'signs of contradiction', as are the angels. Aristotle said that fire on earth is never fire itself, but always something burning, yet the bush on Horeb is not consumed. The chariots above Dothan also displayed supernatural fire, manifesting their angelic nature. Fire kills, but, paradoxically, many ancient religions have seen fire as divinely creative; the fire of life as opposed to the fire of death. The phoenix rises from the ashes. In Greek mythology the artificer Hephaestus, god of fire, wrought Achilles' shield out of the elemental metals, to present a microcosm.[10] In neo-Platonic terms, 'even so is the cosmos wrought by the ever-living divine fire eternally differentiating itself into the many, and the never-ending return movement of the many into itself.'[11] God himself is not fire: 'You have not come [as at Sinai] to what may be touched, a blazing fire, and darkness, and gloom, and a tempest' (Heb. 12:18). Nevertheless, his power will finally burn up what does not conform to his eternal will. '. . . let us offer to God acceptable worship with reverence and awe; for our God is a consuming fire' (ibid. v. 29). Christ said: 'I came to cast fire upon the earth; and would that it were already kindled!' (Luke 12:49). His fire is like the natural forest fires of Australia which make way for regeneration and new life.

We know, too, that flames must go upwards, but divine fire may come down; the angels both ascend and descend, and their miraculous fire comes down upon the sacrifices before arising to heaven. The seraph who brings fire down from God's altar to give true speech to Isaiah prefigures the descent of the Holy Spirit as flames of fire on the apostles at

Pentecost, giving them the gift of tongues. At Pentecost the apostles were enabled to join the prophets and angels as messengers and mediators of the word of God. They were sealed with the signs of wind and fire, signs of the Holy Spirit. We should notice a distinct difference, however, between human mediators and the angels. The apostles and prophets received the sign of fire, divine fire which initiates, purges and sanctifies them to speak God's word. They are raised in a special way above their fellow human beings, but they remain sinners just the same; divine fire does not make them partakers of divinity. Angels, by contrast, themselves carry the supernatural fire, in forms made manifest to human perception. They are the bearers of the sign, who come down so that God may be revealed and people may hear his voice, but they remain spirits, 'of the air'. The prophet is always human, the angels always divine: in each godhead and manhood approximate, but do not unite. The mediation of both prophets and angels thus falls short of the perfect mediation of Christ, in whom Godhead and Manhood not only approximate, but become personally one.[12] In him all mediators find their highest unity, and through his perfect mediation all humankind can partake of divinity and be taken into God.

The giving of the Holy Spirit at Pentecost is the culmination of all previous signs of divine fire. The images that begin with the first flames of creation arrive at Christ as their climax. He is carried in them throughout, it is he they bring forth. And so, Mary, the tree whose virgin leaves were unconsumed by the fire of the Spirit, brought him forth for us, by the message of an angel.

Notes for Part II Chapter 4

[1] The Hebrew verb, frequently translated as 'came upon' (v. 34) actually means 'clothed'; it seems a pity to lose this metaphor in translation; I like the image it evokes.

[2] Ps. 104:4 and Heb. 1:7. In the context of the previous lines of the psalm many translators, in particular recent

ones such as the New Jerusalem Bible, take 'winds' and 'fire' as objects of the verb, e.g. 'You make the clouds your chariot, You walk on the wings of the wind [v. 3]. You make the *winds* your messengers, and *flashing fire* your servants [v. 4]' (*Grail Psalms*). One scholarly commentator supports the LXX translation, and the Greek of Hebrews 1:7, which renders the words in the same order as the Hebrew, as I do here, taking 'angels' and 'ministers' as objects, 'winds' and 'fire' as predicates: 'God commissions his servants to assume the agency or form of flames for his purposes.' (H. Alford, *The Greek Testament*, Vol. IV (J. Rivington, London; Deighton Bell, Cambridge, 1880) on Hebrews, 1:7, p. 20.) AV and R. Knox take the Hebrew word order, AV giving the closest rendering: 'Who maketh his angels spirits, his ministers a flaming fire.' But Alford goes on to say: 'It is evident that *pneumata* must be rendered "winds" and not "spirits" from both the context of the psalm and the correspondence of the two clauses and also from the nature of the subject . . . It could not with any meaning be said that he *makes* them spirits.' (op.cit.)

3   See T. H. Gaster, *Myth, Legend and Custom in the Old Testament* (Harper, London, 1969) p. 230f.

4   *Pace* M. Noth, *Exodus* (SCM, London, 1962).

5   See Gal. 3:19; Deut. 33:19 (LXX); also Josephus, *Antiquities*, 15,5,3; Augustine, *De Trinitate*, 3,11,11: 'It is from God, through the angels, that we learn our most beautiful doctrines, the holiest parts of our law.' (My translation)

6   See *New Jerome Biblical Commentary* (Chapman, London, 1989) p. 234.

7   J. Hastings, ed., *Dictionary of the Bible* (Clark, London, 1898–1909), Strachan, 'Seraphim'.
    (My note) The Hebrew word for 'serpent' is close, giving the idea of lightning's movement, but also an association with a dragon-like creature, such as the guardian *'kerub'*. The consonant shift from s-r-ph to k-r-b, is slight, so the origin of 'cherubim' and 'seraphim' could be one and

the same. (See Brown-Driver-Briggs *Hebrew Lexicon* (Hendrickson, Peabody, Mass., 1979)). However uncertain the title's interpretation may be, the adjective '*saraphim*' is used in Num. 21:6 for the 'fiery' serpents (*nechashim*) in the desert, so the general notion of fiery angelic beings is not entirely misplaced.

[8] See A. Farrer, *The Revelation of St John the Divine* (O.U.P., Oxford, 1964) p. 26.

[9] Rabbi Dr H. Freedman and M. Simon, eds., *Midrash Rabbah* to the Song of Songs, 1,10,2 (Soncino P., London, 1961).

[10] Homer, *Iliad* 18:468f.

[11] G. Casey, 'The Shield of Achilles' in *Echoes* (Rigby and Lewis, Crawley, 1990).

[12] H. Alford, op.cit., p. 13.

PART III

Ministers

Bless the Lord, all his hosts, his ministers that do his will!
(Ps. 103:21)

1. Rescuers

The angel of the Lord encamps around those
who fear him, and delivers them.
(Ps. 34:7)

The one Mediator, who became both a master to be served and the servant of humanity, employs angel mediators to continue his saving work. In the New Testament angels are described as 'ministering spirits, sent forth to serve [*eis diakonian* lit. 'into service']' (Heb. 1:14). This term has particular application to the angelic ministry, not only because of its use as a form of ecclesiastical service, that of a deacon, but for an earlier fund of meanings as well. A recent discussion of service in the Church refers to research on the non-Christian sources of the word '*diakonos*', and concludes that:

> this is a family of words 'designating actions of an in-between kind of people, who operate in an in-between capacity, especially people (or spirits) who implement the intentions or desires of another'. Ambassadors, heralds, couriers, political agents, generals could all be called *diakonoi*; even go-betweens in love affairs; anyone who was charged to speak in another's name or do things on their behalf. There are overtones of the sacred, of mediation between heaven and earth. And where one does have *diakonoi* serving at table, the word refers not so much to their service of the people at the table as to their coming and going between kitchen and table.[1]

Angels can be 'deacons'; their 'in-between capacity' has so far been the subject of this book, and now their function as ministers, or servants, comes to the fore. It is difficult to discuss their ministry on a broad basis because we cannot know how much they are actually doing. What we perceive, or read about, we must believe to be only the tip of the iceberg.[2] Quite apart from the testimony of individuals to angelic ministry in their personal lives, the angels of God must be constantly 'working his purpose out, as year succeeds to year', invisibly and beyond our accountability. Some areas of their ministry have been delineated by Christian tradition, and we may attempt to perceive others from what we have learned of the possible fields of angelic activity. The following chapters will consider their ministry as guardians and guides, and their priestly ministry of worship and praise with its relation to our liturgy and the sacraments of the Church. To begin with, I shall consider the angelic ministries of healing and saving.

Healing and saving

How much did Jesus use angelic assistance in his work on earth? Did he employ angels in his healing miracles? A story in the eighth chapter of Matthew's Gospel bears close examination. A centurion came up to Jesus saying that he had a servant lying at home paralysed. When Jesus offered to come and heal the servant the centurion replied:

> 'Lord, I am not worthy to have you come under my roof; but only say the word, and my servant will be healed. For I am a man under authority, with soldiers under me; and I say to one, "Go", and he goes, and to another; "Come", and he comes, and to my slave "Do this", and he does it.' (Matt. 8:8–9)

Jesus marvelled at the man's faith, even suggesting that it was unique in his experience at that time.

> And to the centurion Jesus said 'Go, be it done for you as you have believed.' And the servant was healed at that very moment. (Matt. 8: 5–13)

The centurion showed a humility that is truly 'worthy', in a human sense; in his position he could command a Jew to do anything he pleased. His reluctance in asking Jesus into his house was part of his faith in him, and a signal courtesy. What exactly did the centurion believe? Perhaps that Jesus was a prophet, a man of God, and that as such he was under the authority of God, just as the centurion was under his immediate superior. And that the command the prophet would give to heal the servant would be obeyed by spiritual powers under the prophet's authority, in the same way that the centurion's soldiers obeyed him. If the centurion's belief, so highly commended by Jesus, was right, then perhaps Christ did use an angel to heal the centurion's servant. The centurion's words are echoed by us in the Eucharist: 'Lord, I am not worthy to receive you, but only say the word and I shall be healed'. When we ask him to say the word, and heal us, we are perhaps opening the way for an angel to act at Christ's word, making us ready in faith to receive Christ himself who will then heal us in the sacrament.

The centurion's graphic account of his exercise of authority offers an image of the authority of God over the angels: 'I say to one, Go, and he goes, and to another, Come and he comes . . .' All the angels in the Bible are carrying out such commands. Many of their appearances are to give assistance, or to rescue. The angel appears at the time of greatest need, as when Hagar and Ishmael are dying of thirst in the desert (Gen. 21; see chapter 2, Part I, above). In the next chapter of Genesis comes the story of the testing of Abraham. Abraham himself obeys the command of God and takes Isaac into the mountains to offer him in sacrifice. It is the voice of an angel that stays Abraham's hand as he is about to kill his son:

The angel of the Lord called to him from heaven, and said, 'Abraham, Abraham!' And he said, 'Here am I.' He said, 'Do not lay your hand on the lad or do anything to him; for now I know that you fear God, seeing you have not withheld your son, your only son, from me.' (Gen. 22:11–12)

This is one of the many examples of the angel speaking both as an angel, and in the voice of God; here the doubling occurs within a single sentence. The angel later gives Abraham God's solemn promise:

> And the angel of the Lord called to Abraham a second time from heaven and said, 'By myself I have sworn, says the Lord, because you have done this, and have not withheld your son, your only son, I will indeed bless you, and I will multiply your descendants as the stars of heaven and as the sand which is on the seashore. And your descendants shall possess the gate of their enemies, and by your descendants shall all the nations of the earth bless themselves, because you have obeyed my voice.' (vv. 15–18)

Robert Alter has pointed out the parallels in these two scenes in Genesis which describe life-threatening trials in the wilderness; the first to Abraham's elder son Ishmael, then to his younger son Isaac.[3] In the first there is a desperate mother, in the second an anguished father, to both of whom an angel calls at the critical moment, and saves. The angel's voice is a source of life in the desert, and a stay of execution on the mountain. In each case the angel gives a promise that the child will be the father of many descendants. The action of the angel reveals not only the unfailing love of God but also his covenant. Abraham is taken to the last bounds of obedience and trust; the angel acts at the very brink of death. Augustine said that the trial of Abraham was to prove the strength of his faith to Abraham himself, rather than to God. The angel called not a second too late; nor too soon, before the test was conclusive. Both stories insist that everything is given by God, and through trust in him.

Earlier in Genesis, after the messengers at Mamre have finally announced Isaac's birth, (see chapter 2, Part II, above) two angels arrive at the city of Sodom, just before its destruction, and save Abraham's nephew, Lot (ch. 19). God has given Abraham a pledge that he will not destroy the city if ten righteous men are found there, but in the event, Lot is apparently the only one. When they are in Lot's house, the angels tell him that the Lord has sent them to destroy Sodom (v. 13). They seem thus to carry a dual function as both rescuing and destroying angels. Their act of rescue takes precedence, however, and when it comes to the destruction of the city we read that '*the Lord* rained on Sodom and Gomorrah brimstone and fire *from the Lord* out of heaven; and *he* overthrew those cities' (vv. 24–5, my emphases). The angels are seen in action in the story as rescuers only. The text shows a familiar shift from angels to God; we should not insist on too rigid an interpretation of it, but it is interesting for this study to see that angels usually exhibit one type of function only.

The two angels arriving at Sodom are greeted by Lot with the address 'My lords [*adonai*] . . .' (v. 2). He recognizes their distinction, even if he does not know they are angels, and constrains them to come into his house. When the Sodomites surround the house, demanding that the men come out to them, Lot is prepared to hand over his daughters rather than see the angels abused. The mob, perhaps in reaction to Lot's known trickery, would break the door down to get at him and the angels. They immediately come to the rescue, drawing Lot back into the house.

> And they struck with blindness the men who were at the door of the house, both small and great, so that they wearied themselves with groping for the door. (v. 11)

Once again the angels intervene in the nick of time, using the weapon of *sanwerim*, the special blindness with which Elisha struck the soldiers at Dothan (see chapter 1, Part I, above). They then set about saving Lot and his family from the imminent destruction of the city. His sons-in-law do not take the situation seriously, so are left behind. Lot, his wife and two daughters linger and have to be dragged out by the angels. Even then Lot will not flee into the wilderness, but begs to be allowed to run to a nearby small city. The angels then speak with one voice, the voice of God:

'Behold, I grant you this favour also, that I will not over-throw the city of which you have spoken. Make haste, escape there, for I can do nothing till you arrive there.' (vv. 21–2)

The angels disappear from the narrative at this point, when, like Jacob leaving Peniel, the sun rises on Lot as he trudges towards the 'little' city, Zoar. Lot's wife cannot resist a glance back at Sodom, in spite of the angels' warning, and she becomes a pillar of salt; by what agency we are not told. The final words of the story are a reminder that everything the angels do is in fact God's doing:

So it was that, when God destroyed the cities of the valley, God remembered Abraham, and sent Lot out of the midst of the overthrow, when he overthrew the cities in which Lot dwelt. (v. 29)

Rescue

The book of Daniel contains two scenes where angels come to the rescue. The young Daniel and three companion Jews are in exile, forced into the service of the King of the Chaldeans. Daniel's three companions refuse to worship a golden image made by King Nebuchadnezzar, so are threatened with death by fire. 'Our God whom we serve is able to deliver us from the burning fiery furnace,' they reply to the king; 'but if not, we will not serve your gods or worship the golden image which you have set up' (Dan. 3:17–18). Azariah, Ananiah and Mishael, to give them their Hebrew names, do not take their rescue for granted, but when they are thrown into the furnace:

the angel of the Lord came down into the oven with Azariah and his fellows, and smote the flame of the fire out of the oven; and made the midst of the furnace as it had been a moist whistling wind, so that the fire touched them not at all, neither hurt nor troubled them. (LXX: The song of the three children: 25–6)[4]

The angel of the Lord appears as a fourth man walking with the others, freely, in the middle of the flames. Nebuchadnezzar can see into the oven (something like a lime kiln?); he describes the fourth man as 'like a son of the gods' (3:25 RSV). The Septuagint gives 'a son of God', and some English translations, following the Greek, read: 'like the Son of God'. Many interpret the event as an actual appearance of Christ, the rescue demonstrating his redemption of the whole human race from the power of death. This interpretation may be valid, but it is preferable, I think, to see the rescuer as an angel. As we know, all angels are of Christ, and work through him, in our salvation. In a poem which speaks of the episode with perfect economy of phrase, Mary Casey has the angel acting in the 'breath of God's Son', but that breath did not come from human lungs until Jesus was born.

> The sparkling stars are angels as are
> white fires of waters cool
> in the burning sun's noon
> as the three holy children
> with their whistling wind in the furnace
> the breath of God's Son[5]

It is possible to see in the furnace the angelic form of a man, doing the timeless work of Christ. The three young men are faithful to God, trusting him to save them, whether their bodies are burned or not. The angel comes so that the sign of God's saving power may be seen by those who have no faith in him. The fire in the furnace, with the coming of the angel, becomes supernatural fire that does not consume the three young men.

Some time after this incident, the next king, Darius, places Daniel over all his presidents and satraps. These leaders and governors, jealous of Daniel's excellence, plan his downfall. The rule of the land is that the king shall be worshipped, but Daniel is known to be praying three times every day to the God of Israel. This is reported to Darius, who is reluctant to condemn Daniel, but is forced to abide by the law. When Darius sends Daniel to the lion pit to meet his death, the king says, 'May your God, whom you serve continually, deliver you' (6:16). This time we do not see the angel. At dawn King Darius goes to the lion pit, calling out in anguish to Daniel, 'O Daniel, servant of the living God, has your God, whom you serve continually, been able to deliver you from the lions?' (v. 20). Daniel is alive; he replies that God sent his angel to shut the lions' mouths, and he is unhurt.

> Then the king was exceedingly glad, and commanded that Daniel be taken up out of the den. So Daniel was taken up out of the den, and no kind of hurt was found upon him, because he had trusted in his God. (v. 23)

Daniel's faith occasions his rescue; Abraham's faith is tested in his obedience; Jesus commended the centurion's faith, and that of many people he had healed. The ministry of angels comes to meet those in need, and it meets first with their faith. Lot's wife looked back; her lack of faith and obedience prevented the angels' saving action for her. She became fixed to the spot; there was to be no going forward or back for her.

There are parallels to the Old Testament rescue stories in the lives of Christ's apostles, as they too struggled to remain faithful, and to spread the gospel, building the Church. The first rescue comes quite early in the book of Acts. The apostles were working together, in the new Christian community, which held them in high esteem. The growing numbers of followers and the healing signs given by the apostles aroused the Jewish authorities to jealousy. They threw the apostles, not into a lion pit, but into the common gaol. Presumably all twelve of the Christian leaders were crowded together in this temporary lock-up.

But at night an angel of the Lord opened the prison doors and brought them out, and said, 'Go and stand in the temple and speak to the people all the words of this Life.' And when they heard this, they entered the temple at daybreak and taught. (Acts 5:19–21)

Without the command of the angel, the apostles might have thought it prudent to hide away for a while after their escape, but they did not hesitate to comply, laying themselves open to further arrest. When questioned they answered, 'We must obey God, rather than men' (v. 29). Their obedience to God was their observance of the angel's directive.

Later Peter was imprisoned by Herod who was taking no chances. He had Peter guarded by sixteen soldiers, in squads of four, for the duration of the Passover Feast.

So Peter was kept in prison, but earnest prayer for him was made to God by the Church. (12:5)

Peter was chained to two soldiers, with others guarding all the doors of the prison. Just before Herod planned to bring him to trial, an angel was sent in the night to rescue him.

A light shone in the cell, and the angel struck Peter on the side and woke him, saying, 'Get up quickly.' And the chains fell off his hands. And the angel said to him, 'Dress yourself and put on your sandals.' And he did so. And he said to him, 'Wrap your mantle around you and follow me.' And he went out, and followed him. (vv. 7–9)

Peter was evidently dazed with sleep and probably stiff from the chains and his discomforts. He had to be told every move he must make. He obeyed automatically, and later admitted that he had thought he was dreaming. The text does not say the angel had human form, only that a light shone in the cell. It was not until Peter had gone past the first and second guards, and through the miraculously opening iron gate leading out into the city, that he came to himself, and realized that he was awake, and the escape real. At that moment the angel left him.

> Peter said, 'Now I am sure that the Lord has sent his angel and rescued me from the hand of Herod and from all that the Jewish people were expecting.' (v. 11)

He went at once to where the believers were gathered, praying for him. The incident that followed is one of those amusing anecdotes that convince by their spontaneity. Peter knocked at the gatehouse of the residence, but when the maid, Rhoda, recognized Peter's voice, she ran off joyfully to tell everyone else, without opening the gate to let him in. Peter had to stand exposed in the street while Rhoda persuaded them that she was not mad, but had really heard Peter's voice. They were so sure that he was locked up in prison that someone suggested it must be 'Peter's angel' whose voice Rhoda had heard. This does not refer to the angel who rescued Peter, but to his guardian angel, as we would now call it.

A third rescue in which an angel played a part is told in Acts 27, when Paul's life was saved in a shipwreck. Paul was a prisoner of the Roman authorities, in custody to save him from Jewish assassins, rather than because of any Roman case against him. As a citizen of Rome from birth, Paul appealed to Caesar, after which the governor Festus had no alternative but to send him to Rome, contrary to his own inclinations. The weather and the season were against a speedy arrival in Italy; after many delays and dangers Paul and his companions and guards found themselves on board an Alexandrian ship in the open sea, having left behind the coast of Crete. (The voyage narrative is written as by an eyewitness; possibly Luke was one of the group.)

> And when neither sun nor stars appeared for many a day, and no small tempest lay on us, all hope of our being saved was at last abandoned. (27:20)

Paul, the prisoner, spoke with confidence and authority:

> 'Men, you should have listened to me, and should not have set sail from Crete, and incurred this injury and loss. I now bid you to take heart; for there will be no loss of life among you, but only of the ship. For this very night there stood by me an angel of the God to whom I belong and whom I worship, and he said to me, "Do not be afraid, Paul; you must stand before Caesar; and lo, God has granted you all those who sail with you." So take heart, men, for I have faith in God that it will be exactly as I have been told. But we shall have to run aground on some island.' (vv. 21–6)

When they finally ran aground on the rocks of Malta, two weeks later, the ship broke up, and the soldiers were about to kill the prisoners who might have escaped. 'But the centurion, wishing to save Paul, kept them from carrying out their purpose . . . And so it was that all escaped to land' (vv. 43–4). The centurion, having been in Paul's company throughout the hazards of the voyage, knew he was a man of God. The angel's message had undoubtedly given all those on board new heart, and from then on Paul had maintained an authoritative role. The turning-point was God's intervention by his angel. Paul said, 'an angel *stood by me* . . .'

Notes for Part III Chapter 1

1   Timothy Radcliffe OP, 'As one who serves', in *The Tablet*, 11.7.92, referring to John Collins, *Diakonia, Interpreting the Ancient Sources* (O.U.P., Oxford, 1992).

2   A doctor in Holland recently decided to make a private survey of people's experiences of angels. He asked each of his patients a simple question, such as 'Have you ever seen or felt the presence of an angel?' The answers were surprising; a large number of the patients affirmed experience of angelic assistance or intervention in their lives. The outcome of the survey is published as a book,

which has been translated into English: H. C. Moolenbergh, *A Handbook of Angels*, trans. A. Marix-Evans (London, 1984).

3   R. Alter, *The Art of Biblical Narrative* (Basic Books, New York, 1981) pp. 181–2.
4   'The song of the three children' is the title given to this deutero-canonical section of the book of Daniel, published in the Jerusalem Bible as Daniel 3:24–97. The translation I have used is from *The Septuagint with Apocrypha in Greek and English*, ed. L. Benton (Bagster, London, 1851).
5   Mary Casey, from 'A Meditation on Angels' in *The Clear Shadow* (Rigby and Lewis, Crawley, 1992) p. 140.

2. The Book of Tobit

Therefore, when he went to seek a man,
he found Raphael, that was an angel.
(Tobit 5:4)

In the book of Tobit the angel Raphael exemplifies the ministries of angels in healing, rescuing, guarding and guiding. While it has been suggested that angels do not generally display more than one attribute or function at a time, all these roles are played by Raphael in the story of young Tobias who is unknowingly accompanied by an angel in his journey from Nineveh to Ecbatana and back. This is the only scriptural appearance of Raphael in the Christian canon. Raphael announces himself, at the end of Tobit as 'one of the seven angels who stand ever ready to enter the presence of the glory of the Lord' (12:15, JB). The name Raphael has some connection with healing, though it is hard to give a direct translation from the Hebrew; the nearest would be 'God heals'.

The book of Tobit was written between the second and fourth centuries BC, by a Jew living, most probably, in Egypt.[1] The Greek texts may derive from an Aramaic original, but they show variations, and scholars are divided as to which texts could be earlier. Jerome included his Latin translation of a late Aramaic version among the deutero-canonical books of the Old Testament. These have been generally accepted as scriptural by the Roman Catholic and Eastern Orthodox Churches, but many Protestant Churches, while accepting that they have special value, see them as outside the canon of scripture. The Anglican Church prizes them for devotional and inspirational reading, but maintains their apocryphal status. I shall quote from an English translation of the shorter Greek text, Codex Vaticanus, included in the Septuagint.[2]

Tobit advances the representation of angels far beyond anything else in the Old Testament, and the New Testament also. Belief in angels had taken a strong hold in Jewish tradition during the exile in Babylon, possibly as a result of Persian influences. After the return from exile in the sixth century BC, angels multiply in Jewish literature, where they are given names and characteristics, together with functions both good and evil. This is why Raphael displays several roles in the story, and why he appears so convincingly human. Nevertheless, the underlying message of the book can assist our attempts to discover the nature of angelic activity, partly by contrast with the greater simplicity of the other texts under discussion, and partly by looking for the key aspects of Raphael's work in the story.

Raphael is seen in opposition to Asmodeus, an evil spirit. The name 'Asmodeus' (or *Ashmedai*, probably derived from the Persian *Aeshma daeva*, an evil spirit in Zoroastrian mythology[3]) appears in the book of Tobit for the first time in Jewish literature. Later he became an important and sinister figure. In *The Testament of Solomon* (AD 300) he claims 'My role is to conspire against newly-weds and prevent them making love.'[4] Raphael provides Tobias with the means to drive the evil spirit from the bridal chamber, whereupon Raphael himself defeats him. Although this is the turning-point of the story, Raphael's other roles are actually more fundamental to the overall significance of the book, which is that God is always with his people; in their suffering and their fear, in their homes and on their travels, God sends his angel to defeat evil, to heal, to guard and guide. Because of the nature of the narrative, it is legitimate to treat it as literature with form, direction, and plot, and the characters as revealing personal changes with the development of the story, but without imposing vague twentieth-century ideas on a book that is a blend of folklore and sacred scripture.

The story is set in the eighth century BC at the time of Assyrian oppression of the Jews. Exiled in Nineveh, Tobit is upright and God-fearing. He makes it his particular concern, in spite of persecution, to bury the bodies of his own people killed by the Assyrians and left lying in the streets of Nineveh. One night he returns home from a burial, and lies down to sleep by the courtyard wall of his house.

> 'My face was uncovered, and I knew not that there were sparrows in the wall, and mine eyes being open, the sparrows muted warm dung into mine eyes, and a whiteness came upon mine eyes, and I went to the physicians but they helped me not'. (Tobit 2:10)

For several years the blind Tobit lives on in Nineveh, his wife Anna taking in work for their living. One day Tobit accuses her of stealing a kid that she has been given as an extra wage. When he repeats his charge she turns on him, saying, 'Where are thine alms and thy righteous deeds now?' (2:14). Tobit goes away from the house to weep in remorse and grief. He prays that God should end his life.

On the same day, in the city of Ecbatana at the house of Raguel, a cousin of Tobit, Raguel's daughter Sarah also prays for death. She is in the clutches of the spirit Asmodeus, who has killed her seven bridegrooms, each on the night of their marriage to Sarah. When her maid accuses her of strangling the husbands herself, Sarah falls into despair: 'O Lord, take me out of the earth that I may hear no more reproach' (3:13). The simultaneous prayers of Tobit and Sarah:

> were heard before the majesty of the great God. And Raphael was sent to heal them both; that is to scale away the whiteness of Tobit's eyes, and to give Sarah the daughter of Raguel for a wife to Tobias, the son of Tobit, and to bind Asmodeus the evil spiri.t (3:16–17)

The reader is told the eventual outcome of the story in order to see clearly that Raphael is central to the family's salvation. His healing work is a making whole, a bringing together of all the people involved. The coincidence of time signifies supernatural intervention, and Raphael's offering the prayers to God effects a united movement by Sarah and Tobit, though they are many miles apart:

> The self-same time came Tobit home and entered his house, Sarah the daughter of Raguel came down from her upper chamber. (3:17)

Their new life begins. Tobit remembers some money which he had left with a relative in the city of Rages. Thinking that he may be granted his dying wish, Tobit decides to send his son Tobias to collect the money in case it should remain unclaimed. He tells Tobias to go and find a trustworthy companion for the journey.

> Therefore when he went out to seek a man, he found Raphael that was an angel. (5:4)

This succinct statement is Raphael's entry on stage.

> But he [Tobias] knew not; and he said to him, 'Canst thou go with me to Rages?' (5:5)

From this moment on the narrative is rich with ironies. 'Can' Raphael go to Rages? asks the unknowing Tobias. 'To whom the angel replied, I will go with thee . . .' Here is God's reply to Moses, Gideon, Jacob, and all of us. He is with his people always. Connections with other angelic visitations in scripture are made next, when Tobit meets Raphael, and asks for his name. 'Azarias' is given as his alias for the time being. The Hebrew name 'Azariah' means 'Yahweh has helped'.

> So they were well pleased. Then said Tobit to Tobias, 'Prepare thyself for the journey. Go with this man, and God which dwelleth in heaven prosper your journey, and the angel of God keep you company.' So they went forth both, and the young man's dog with them. (5:16)

The mention of the dog which accompanies them throughout is similar in appeal to Tobit's ingenuous invocation of the angel of God. The reader is repeatedly made aware of two worlds, the homely and the sublime, that come together in the story.

On the way to Rages Tobias is washing in the river Tigris when he is attacked by a great fish, which tries to kill him. At Raphael's command he catches the fish. Tobias is then directed to remove the heart, liver and gall; they are to be the sacraments of Raphael's healing, though Tobias is told little of this as yet. The heart and liver will be burned under the nose of Asmodeus, who will flee from the 'fishy fume'. They are symbols of life: the life of the fish, and the life of Tobias which the fish nearly took. They will save the life of Sarah also, to produce further life for the family. The heart and liver will be spiritualized, turned into smoke and scent, putting the demon to flight when he breathes the incense of life. The fish is evidently associated with the crocodile; it was believed in Egypt that the smell of smoke from a crocodile's liver cured epilepsy, which was commonly attributed to possession by evil spirits. The dung and gall of the crocodile were used for leucoma.[5] Raphael tells Tobias that the gall is good 'to anoint a man that hath a whiteness in his eyes, and he shall be healed' (6:8).

As Tobias, Raphael and the dog approach Rages, Raphael tells Tobias that they will first lodge in Ecbatana with his father's cousin, Raguel.[6] With the arrival at Raguel's house the narrative plays on a delayed recognition of Tobias by his father's cousin, prefiguring the delay until the end of the story of Raphael's revelation of his true identity:

Raguel said to his wife Edna, 'How like is this young man to Tobit my cousin!' And Raguel asked them, 'From whence are you come, brethren?' To whom they said, 'We are of the sons of Naphtali, which are captives in Nineveh.' Then he said to them, 'Do you know Tobit our kinsman?' And they said, 'We know him.' Then he said, 'Is he in good health?' And they said, 'He is alive, and in

157

good health.' And Tobias said, 'He is my father.' Then Raguel leaped up, and kissed him, and wept, and blessed him, and said to him, 'Thou art the son of an honest and good man.' But when he had heard that Tobit was blind, he was sorrowful, and wept. And likewise Edna his wife and Sarah his daughter wept. (7:2–8)

Before they sit down to eat Raphael asks Raguel for Sarah, to be Tobias' bride. Raguel tells them the whole truth, but Tobias replies, 'I will eat nothing till we agree and swear to one another' (7:11). Raguel brings Sarah, and says to Tobias:

'Behold, take her after the law of Moses, and lead her away to thy father.' And he blessed them, and called Edna his wife, and took paper, and did write an instrument of covenants, and sealed it. Then they began to eat. (7:13–15)

Sarah goes to the bridal chamber, where her mother weeps over her, then Tobias is called to go in to her.

And as he went, he remembered the words of Azarias, and took the ashes of the perfumes, and put the heart and liver of the fish thereon, and made a smoke therewith. The which smell when the evil spirit had smelled, he fled into the utmost parts of Egypt, and the angel bound him. (8:2–3)

Asmodeus, spirit of death, flees from the breath of life. Raphael binds him; the opposite of the release of healing. Unusually, the angel has used Tobias as his agent, to drive off the demon. Tobias has to go in alone to make the smoke; his trust is all the greater for his ignorance of the identity of Azarias, and Raphael acts with all his power in the impetus produced by the free co-operation of Tobias.

Tobias and Sarah pray together. Their prayer is essential to the healing process; it places them in the hands of God

158

who alone holds the truth. At the end of the prayer Tobias says:

'And now, O Lord, I take this my sister not for lust but for truth; ordain mercy for me, that we may grow old together.' And she said, 'Amen'. So they slept both that night. (8:7–8)

While the couple sleep there is activity in the household below. Raguel is digging a grave for Tobias, just in case. He dare not go himself in the morning to see if Tobias is dead or alive, but sends a maid:

So the maid opened the door, and went in, and found them both asleep, and came forth, and told them that he was alive. (8:13–14)

Raguel sings a hymn of praise to God, orders the grave to be filled in and sets about the wedding festivities. The feast will last for fourteen days, so in order not to delay the return to Nineveh, Tobias requests Azarias to go on to Rages and collect the money from Gabael. Raphael complies, bringing Gabael with him to share in the family occasion. Tobias has increased in stature through all his experiences. He can take command, and send Azarias off with an assured tone. Tobias does not know that he is commanding an angel; had he known from the first the true nature of his companion he might not have achieved this growth.

Tobit and Anna are still in ignorance at home. As the entourage travels back to Nineveh Raphael reminds Tobias that his father is still blind; the healing work is not yet complete. He tells Tobias to have the fish's gall ready. He is to go ahead of the caravan and greet his father. 'I know, Tobias,' says Raphael, 'that thy father will open his eyes.' Tobit's eyes will be strained open in his intense longing to see his son. Tobias is to take the opportunity to pour the gall into his father's eyes. Anna sees Tobias, Raphael and the dog approaching. Sarah and the rest have waited further back.

Then Anna ran forth, and fell upon the neck of her son, and said unto him, 'Seeing I have seen thee, from henceforth I am content to die.' And they both wept. Tobit also went forth toward the door, and stumbled; but his son ran unto him, and took hold of his father, and he strake off the gall on his father's eyes, saying, 'Be of good hope, my father,' and when his eyes began to smart, he rubbed them; and the whiteness scaled away from the corners of his eyes; and when he saw his son he fell upon his neck. (11:9–14)

All that remains is for Raphael to reveal his true identity. The angel takes Tobit and his son aside, first exhorting them always to praise God. Then he says:

I will keep nothing from you, for while it is good to keep the secrets of the king, it is honourable to reveal the works of God. When thou didst pray, and Sarah thy daughter-in-law, I did bring the remembrance of your prayers before the Holy One . . . I am Raphael, one of the seven holy angels which present the prayers of the saints and which go in and out before the glory of the Holy One.' Then they were troubled, and fell on their faces, for they feared. But he said to them, 'Fear not, for it shall go well with you.' (12:11–12 and 15–17)

Even as everything is made clear, they are troubled and afraid. So we can see why the fact of Raphael's identity had been kept from them until now; they would not have been able to take it. Only when their lives have been put in order and they are cured can they possibly receive such momentous knowledge, and still they are troubled by it, afraid of the divine origin of the figure who stands before them, and of God's hand upon them. Raphael goes on to say:

All these days I did appear to you, but I did neither eat nor drink, ye did see a vision. (12:19)

The writer is anxious to point out that Raphael was always truly angelic, his human body was assumed for the part played on earth.

> 'Now therefore give thanks, for I go up to him who sent me; but write all these things which are done in a book.' And when they arose, they saw him no more. Then they confessed the great and wonderful works of God, and how the angel of the Lord had appeared to them. (12:20–2)

Tobit and Tobias are still on their knees in reverence when the angel disappears suddenly. He has instructed them to write down the story of what has happened. All the works of God are a great story made up of lesser stories, and in them, in miniature, the highest truths are told. Raphael, in the story of the book of Tobit, reveals God's constant presence, and exemplifies the ministry of angels in great and small affairs of human life.

Notes for Part III Chapter 2

[1] See D. C. Simpson, 'Tobit', in R. D. Charles ed., *Apocrypha and Pseudepigrapha*, Vol. I (O.U.P., Oxford, 1913) p. 186. Other scholars uphold the more recent date, i.e. 200–180 BC, because of various historical details in the narrative.

[2] Edition: London, 1851.

[3] D. S. Russell, *The Method and Measure of Jewish Apocalyptic* (SCM, London, 1964) p. 260.

[4] See J. C. Dancy ed., *The Shorter Books of the Apocrypha* (C.U.P., Cambridge, 1972) and 'Angel of Death', *Encyclopaedia Judaica* (Keter Publishing House, Jerusalem, 1971).

[5] Simpson op.cit., p. 186.

[6] The author's ignorance of eastern geography is a strong argument in favour of his being an exile in the west, according to Simpson. That the Tigris flowed between Nineveh and Media was an idea common in Greek and Roman standard geographical treatises; that Ecbatana

was situated in a plain, near Rages, was a western fallacy repeated in Diodorus. Other pointers are the identification of the fish with the crocodile, and the binding of Asmodeus in Upper Egypt, 'the veritable dumping ground of wickedness and sin, exactly as Zechariah had regarded Babylon, the land of exile' (Simpson op.cit., p. 185).

3. Guardians and Guides

*'See that you do not despise one of these little ones; for I tell you
that in heaven their angels always behold the face of my Father who
is in heaven.'*

(MATT. 18:10)

The angel 'stood by' Paul in the ship, and was instrumental in saving him and others from drowning. Raphael remained with Tobias on his journey, there and back. There are angels, we are told, who stand by us continuously, this being their sole function. Christian tradition cites the saying of Jesus quoted above as the basis for its belief in a personal angel for every individual, and the concept is widespread, both in time and place. A salutation among French peasants as late as the nineteenth century was *'Bonjour à vous et votre compagnon'* ('Good day to you and your companion'),[1] demonstrating the persistence of customary acknowledgement of the presence of companion spirits. The idea emerges in many ancient cultures, particularly among the Greeks, who used the word *'daimon'* for such spirits, among other uses of the word. While our understanding of guardian angels owes much to the concept of the personal *daimon* in Hellenistic tradition, the two should not be confused. The Greeks spoke of a man or woman's *daimon* as a moving force within them, which manifested itself in their emotions and behaviour. Irrational impulses might be attributed to the *daimon*. It was a part of the person, but had a life and energy of its own. Christian belief in guardian angels does not arise from a desire to explain the workings of the human mind or will, but out of a desire to understand the workings of grace. Alongside this search run innumerable strands of folklore, legend, and personal experience of the existence of accompanying spirits. The most obvious symbol of this is the shadow, that evocatively mysterious figure who, aping our movements, also leaps, dances and plays tricks of appearance and disappearance with the changes of sunlight. The literary motif of the *doppelgänger* has been employed by countless writers. Sometimes the mysterious double is a counterpart of a character, sometimes a spirit or shadow that may or may not resemble a character. The spontaneous reaction of Peter's fellow Christians to his unexpected appearance indicates how basic was the idea of a personal angel who resembled its charge in voice.

Guardian angels

In Christian tradition there is nothing chancy or fickle about these accompanying spirits. Christ's words in Matthew's Gospel imply the presence of personal angels. Thomas Aquinas wrote: 'To watch over each person a separate angel is deputed. The reason is that the guardianship of angels is a particular execution of Divine providence concerning mankind.'[2] Jesus spoke of the angels while he had a child at his knee, and warned against despising one of these 'little ones'. He referred, surely, not only to that child but to all the children of God. Humanity is one whole, the entire 'flock'; the verse quoted is followed by the parable of the lost sheep. 'It is not the will of my Father that one of these little ones should perish' (Matt. 18:14). Each one has therefore been given an angel, we believe, under the command of the Shepherd; 'for the Son of Man came to save the lost.' (So reads v. 11, which is omitted from some manuscripts.)

The angels attendant upon every single person 'always behold the face of my Father who is in heaven.' Christ prefaces these words with the phrase: 'For I tell you (*lego gar humin*) . . .' which carries nearly the same weight as his 'Amen I say to you', or 'Truly I say to you'. His following words must always be taken particularly seriously; often they are 'revelations of the unseen world of glory'.[3] Each guardian angel is always in the presence of God. Where now is the superiority of the seven 'angels of the presence'? Christ said everyone has an angel that is in fact as great as the highest archangel.

'In heaven they always behold the face of my Father in heaven.' Heaven must not be imagined as a far-away place, where our guardian angels remain as ambassadors for their wards on earth. Jesus said, 'the kingdom of God is within you' (Luke 17:21, AV). Guardian angels do not travel between us and God, they 'always behold the face of my Father', and as Augustine wrote: 'God is nearer to the soul than it is to itself.'[4] The personal ministry of guardian angels does not mean that God is distanced from us. Their operations take place in the same closeness by which the Holy Trinity dwells in each of us, and we in the Holy Trinity. The personal ministry of guardian angels is an extension of the deep mystery of our personal relationship with God. Its reality can be experienced, as can the love of God. Our trust in God is also trust in his providence of help from his invisible creation. The more we are open to its reality the more we will receive from it, and a reciprocal process can begin; for we are able to give to the angels from our store of spiritual gifts: love, wonder, appreciation and joy.

The Liturgy of the Orthodox Church has a prayer in the Litany before the Communion of the Faithful: 'For an angel of peace, a faithful guide, a guardian of our souls and bodies, let us entreat the Lord.' Nicholas Cabasilas, a fourteenth-century theologian, comments: 'We pray for a guardian angel, not that one may be given to us, since each of us has one from the moment of birth, but that it may be active and may fulfil its task, that it may protect us and lead us in the right way, and may not, angered by our sins, desert us.'[5] Each one of us has a guardian angel from the moment of birth – or even, perhaps, before birth. My guardian angel must be created exclusively for its function; I think it would be erroneous to imagine an arbitrary selection of angelic spirits to exist in relation to human souls. We have emerged together from the beginning to reach fulfilment at the end. Dwelling together in Christ's love, we are moved together deeper into him. My angel is so close to me, so much part of me, while still being an angel, that it might have some imprint of my personality. The early Christians thought 'Peter's angel' had his voice; my angel has my voice, my way of being. Perhaps its task is to draw me towards the perfection demanded of me by Christ: 'You must be perfect, as your heavenly Father is perfect' (Matt. 5:48). The angel may know, and represent that perfection, which will be completed when all is one in God. No wonder the angels rejoiced at the Incarnation, to know the arrival on earth of the one mediator who would make possible the union of humankind with God. For my angel can only know me through him, with him, and in him; and I can know my angel no other way but in the Holy Trinity, and as part of my self as God knows me. He has given me an angel to guard my very self. A remarkable book called *Talking with Angels* relates a series of dialogues between four young Hungarians and their angels, which took place in 1943–4. One of the angels is heard to say: 'God created you after my image.' Gitta records that she was touched deeply, thinking, 'I exist in the image of my angel!' The angels in this book teach their four how to find their true selves in God, even in the ravaging horrors of war which they faced with incredible courage and hope. Three of them, who were Jews, died in the Nazi holocaust, proving an inspiration to all those around them, right up to the end.[6]

Those who believe in angels will know that we are surrounded by them; the invisible creation permeates the visible and gathers it together, so that we cannot separate ourselves from its continuous operation, but the relation of the human soul to its own guardian angel is closer and more intense than any other mode of relation within the created universe. The birth, death and resurrection of Christ reveal that God's highest intention is to bring the whole human race into himself through Christ. Guardian angels have this single task and their power is directly the power of salvation in Christ. They cannot fail, ultimately, even if their life in the soul for which they are created is never acknowledged by that soul; they live and work there for they cannot do anything else. That soul is their life, in relation to God.

Intercessors

Therefore my angel necessarily participates in my prayer. Our guardian angels are those nearest to us in our prayer, but all angels engage in intercession. Raphael tells Tobit and Sarah that he brought the remembrance of their prayers before the Holy One (Tobit 12:12). The very nature of angels as mediators entails the work of intercession. To intercede is, literally, to go between one person and another; it means to plead with one for another. In the book of Job the word 'interpreter' (Hebrew *melitz*) is used for an angel interceding for Job:

> If there be a messenger with him, an interpreter, one among a thousand, to show unto a man his uprightness: then he is gracious to him, and saith, Deliver him from going down into the pit: I have found a ransom. (Job 33:23–4, AV)

These verses (a very difficult and obscure passage) are often quoted as expressing the belief, at the time the book was written, in angelic intercession. Elihu, one of Job's 'comforters', is declaring that if, instead of trying to stand up for himself before God, Job had an angel, an interpreter, he would be shown his true position. Then there would be a possibility of atonement, and then a person might pray to God himself, and be saved. The angel not only interprets the human cry of despair, he shows the lost the way of righteousness, freely making atonement and pleading their deliverance to God. He is a mediator who takes upon himself the ransom for human salvation. He prefigures Christ.

Jesus said to his disciples, in John's Gospel:

> 'the hour is coming when I shall no longer speak to you in figures but tell you plainly of the Father. In that day you will ask in my name; and I do not say to you that I shall pray the Father for you; for the Father himself loves you, because you have loved me and believed that I came from the Father.' (John 16:25–7)

167

He is here explaining the nature of his intercession for us, which makes possible our fullness of communion with him in the Father by the Holy Spirit. He says, 'I do not say to you that *I shall pray to the Father for you'* – as if you had no relation with the Father yourselves – 'for the Father himself loves you, *because* you have loved me and believed . . .' His intercession ensures our entry into the relationship of love and mercy which is the whole mind of the Father towards humanity, and especially towards those whose love and faith in the Son turn them towards him. Christ is telling us that our relation to God through him and our relation directly with God are one and the same. In that communion the intercession of angels is implicated as an active constituent of Christ's continual intercession. Their mediation can be understood only from the point of its source.

To think always of angels as 'carrying our prayers to God' is to weaken the sense of this essential communion. Raphael's words in Tobit have led on to further disjunctive images in, for instance, the book of Revelation, where angels bear 'golden bowls of incense which are the prayers of the saints' (Rev. 5:8). The angels are seen as detached from the prayer which has become a thing to be carried. Revelation includes letters written to seven young Christian churches, and the letters are addressed to the angels of these churches. The writer understands each church to have a guardian angel. If there are guardian angels for every group of Christians wherever they may be, then the prayer of each group will be the first concern of its angel, and the angel will have a very close association with the group, a sort of 'kindred' spirit, guiding and guarding it as a member of the body of Christ. With regard to personal prayer, our own angel relates to the deepest meaning of the prayer of each one of us and is operative in its expression. There is no action more fitting to the angels than this; it is of their very nature, and all the angels are constantly in a state of prayer before God and with us. Their intercession strengthens the bond of love uniting us with God, because they are an inseparable part of that bond, in which they have their being.

Guides for the journey

Raphael is both guardian and guide to Tobias on his journey. The book of Tobit is the story of that journey which takes Tobias out of childhood into adulthood. The image of a journey is a fundamental one for human life. We are pilgrims on this earth; 'Here we have no lasting city, but we seek the city that is to come' (Heb. 13:14). The most ancient stories and myths tell of journeys; from their very beginning human beings have known that they are travellers, and we learn to understand this by 'making' in song and story journeys which end, having places of arrival. The word 'travel' shares its roots with 'travail'; humanity's journey is its toil, its pain. The destination of the mythic journey is home, the place of rest. The human soul carries within it the call of home; the call to return to God who is our beginning and our end. 'Our hearts are restless till they find their rest in you', said Augustine.

The stories that tell of the origins of the Jewish nation are stories of journeys. Abram is told by the voice of God: 'Go from your country and your kindred and your father's house to the land that I will show you' (Gen. 12:1). Abram and Sarai travel from the north to the land of Canaan, first going right down to Egypt and back again. But Abram will never feel at home in Canaan, and when, much later, he wishes to find a wife for his son Isaac, Abraham (as he is called then) sends a servant back to his northern country, rather than have his son marry a Canaanite. Abraham knows that his servant will have an angel guide for the journey, so he says to the servant:

> 'The Lord, the God of heaven, who took me from my father's house and from the land of my birth, and who spoke to me and swore to me "To your descendants I will give this land," he will send his angel before you, and you shall take a wife for my son from there.' (Gen. 24:7)

Isaac's son, Jacob, also travels; at the end of Jacob's life, when blessing his own sons, he too speaks of the angel guardian and guide 'who has kept me from all harm' (see chapter 3, Part I, above). These journeys culminate in the exodus from slavery in Egypt of the entire company of the descendants of Abraham, Isaac and Jacob. The Israelites then begin yet another journey, of forty years' duration, arriving once more in Canaan, the promised land. Again the angel of the Lord will lead them:

'Behold, I send my angel before you, to guard you on the way and to bring you to the place I have prepared.' (Exod. 23:20)

The angel appears to the Israelites as a pillar of cloud by day, and a pillar of fire by night. At the beginning the angel protects the Israelites from the Egyptians. They have camped for the night, before reaching the Red Sea:

The angel of God who went before the host of Israel moved and went behind them; the pillar of cloud moved from before them and stood behind them, coming between the host of Egypt and the host of Israel. (Exod. 14:19–20)

The Israelites are thus screened from the pursuing enemy who does not approach through the thick mist. After Moses parts the Red Sea at God's command and the people cross safely over, their journey takes them through desert and wilderness, for 'forty years'. That God should send angels as guides to people travelling from one place to another is appropriate to the angelic nature. The angels are there to accompany, save and direct, acting as a connection between the starting-point and the terminus of the journey. The journey of human life begins and ends in God; the angels, always in God, guide us through. The Israelites are constantly attended by angels on their desert journey, whether they realize it or not. The desert experience symbolizes the loneliness of the human race apparently abandoned by God. The angel of the pillar of fire, going ahead to give the Israelites light in the dark, is a sign of the 'light' of God's care for his people, and the angel of the pillar of cloud, that never leaves them, likewise represents God himself. The human journey will always include periods of desert or wilderness. The first book of Kings tells how Elijah, like the children of Israel, flees into the desert from his enemy, Queen Jezebel:

He went a day's journey into the wilderness, and came and sat down under a broom tree; and he asked that he might die, saying, 'It is enough; now, O Lord, take away my life, for I am no better than my fathers.' And he lay down and slept under a broom tree, and behold, an angel touched him, and said to him, 'Arise and eat.' And he looked, and behold, there was at his head a cake baked on hot stones and a jar of water. And he ate and drank, and lay down again. And the angel of the Lord came again a second time, and touched him, and said, 'Arise and eat, else the journey will be too great for you.' And he arose, and ate and drank, and went in the strength of that food forty days and forty nights to Horeb the mount of God. (1 Kgs 19:4–8)

Moses had also spent 'forty days and forty nights' on the mountain; the period of 'forty days' echoes the 'forty years' of the Israelites' wandering in the desert. The number is taken up again by the Gospel writers; Jesus spent 'forty days' in the wilderness. His experience is thus linked with the stories of Moses and Elijah. All these episodes focus, at some point, on God's provision of food and water for the wanderers. The Israelites drink from the rock at Horeb, and eat quails and manna (which is referred to later as 'the bread of the angels', Ps. 78:25) (Exod. 16:13; 17:6). Jesus is tempted to make food for himself out of stones, the temptation being to base his ministry on such miracles; *Matthew* and *Mark* tell us that having overcome the temptations, angels 'ministered to him'. Presumably the angels gave Jesus food and drink, as an angel does for Elijah in the wilderness. In 1 Kings Elijah's angel is attentive and courteous; not only does it provide attractive food, in the 'cake baked on hot stones', but it returns to encourage Elijah to eat and drink more, to give him strength to continue his journey. The angel knows that Elijah's journey will be of 'forty days" duration, ending in the cave on Horeb, where God comes to him.

In the New Testament the prophet John the Baptist wandered in the desert, feeding on 'locusts and wild honey' (Mark 1:6). His wilderness journey prepared him to return and proclaim the One who was to come. Jesus, too, travelled continuously throughout his public ministry. 'Foxes have holes, and birds of the air have nests; but the Son of man has nowhere to lay his head,' he said (Luke 9:58). He meant that he had left home in order to preach his gospel, but as so often, his words also carry a wider significance: people, as opposed to animals and birds, do not belong to the earth but must travel through it as strangers and pilgrims. Christ's birth came about during a journey, and was greeted by some mysterious travellers from the east, who had journeyed a great way to find the new-born King. They symbolize the arrival of the Gentiles to join the Christian pilgrimage, and therefore represent all of us, non-Jews, who have been led by the light of a star, or an angel, to look for Christ. As the poet David Jones puts it, the story of the magi and their caravan is

> Our van,
>   where *we* come in:
> not our advanced details now, but us and all our baggage.[7]

You and I, journeying to find Christ here and now. The 'journey' of life is not merely the stuff of fairy tales, it is real for every one of us. All our travail is travelling; human life is the movement of inner growth marked by personal experience, as well as our physical movement in the living and moving world.

Christ took on our journey when he became one of us. He grew from embryo to manhood, and he grew into the perfect Son of God through travail (cf. Heb. 2:10). Nearly at the end of his journey he said to his disciples: 'You know the way where I am going.' But Thomas said at once, 'Lord, we do not know where you are going, how can we know the way?' Jesus replied; 'I am the way, and the truth, and the life; no one comes to the Father, but by me' (John 14:4–6). In laying down his human and divine life for us he became both the way and the guide, leading us into God. This is the way of each human journey; and every angelic action finds its direction through Christ, to guide humankind together with all creation along that way.

Notes for Part III Chapter 3

[1] E. B. Tylor, *Primitive Culture.* Quoted in T. H. Gaster and J. G. Frazer, *Myth, Legend and Custom in the Old Testament* (Harper, London, 1961) p. 213.
[2] *Summa Theologica*, 1a, 113, 2.
[3] H. Alford, *The Greek Testament*, Vol. I (J. Rivington, London; J. Deighton, Cambridge, 1880) p. 413.
[4] *Enarrationes in Psalmos*, LXXXIV.
[5] From *A Commentary on the Divine Liturgy*, trans. J. M. Hussey and D. A. McNulty (SPCK, London, 1960) p. 87.
[6] Gitta Mallasz, *Talking with Angels* (Daimon Verlag, Zurich, 1992) p. 44.
[7] David Jones, *Anathemata* (Faber, London, 1972) p. 190.

4. Angels' Song

In the presence of the angels I will praise you,
I will adore before your holy temple.
(PSALM 138:1–2: THE GRAIL 137)

The angels' worship is their highest service to God; in it their ministry finds its origin and purpose. In Isaiah's vision of heaven the seraphim call to one another in the words of a great hymn of praise, and at the sound of it 'the foundations of the thresholds' shake and the house is filled with smoke. The Church takes up this hymn in the liturgy which is the highest earthly service to God. We could wish that the foundations of the churches might shake at the sound of our praise, and the buildings be completely filled, not only with the smoke of incense, but also the prayer it signifies. The angels give us constant assistance in our worship, helping to make it more nearly in tune with theirs, and the song of angels would surely be a most beautiful sound, if we were to hear it.

In the Middle Ages and later it was a general opinion that the music of angels could not be heard by those in a state of sin, and some said that the ability to hear it was lost in the fall from Paradise.

> . . . the heavenly tune, which none can hear
> of human mould, with grosse unpurged ear.[1]

The idea that grossness of flesh prevents us from hearing the music of the heavens was a medieval inheritance from Platonism, and so embraces, anachronistically, pre-Christian concepts of angels' song. Plato saw the movements of each planet and star as governed by a spiritual or angelic 'intelligence' which was the innate being of the heavenly sphere itself; angels were 'the movers of the stars'. Platonists maintained that the order of the heavens, kept by the angelic spheres, is so harmonious that it produces a beautiful music, each sphere sounding its own note. Walter Hilton, writing in the fourteenth century, describes how we may hear angels' song, but only when we have been cleansed of sensuality and raised above earthly things:

> No soul may truly feel the angels' song nor heavenly sound unless it is in perfect charity. And not all that are in perfect charity feel it, but only that soul that is purified in the fire of love of God, that all earthly savour is burnt out of it and all obstacles between the soul and the cleanness of angels are broken down and put away from it. Then may he sing a new song, and may he hear a blissful heavenly sound and angels' song without deceit or feigning.[2]

Perhaps a new awareness of the reality of angels can bring about a silencing of twentieth-century noise for those who desire to hear angels' song. Such a silent awareness and reciprocity could be the new song we sing, 'restoring with a new verse the ancient rhyme'.[3] So Walter Hilton and others are right to say we must be purged before we can know the angels' song; purged of images and words, and ready to enter into their silent harmony.

The Church's liturgy

Taking part in the Church's liturgy, however, is the surest way to hear angelic music and sounds. The liturgy is 'a clear and fundamental locus for the presence of angels not simply as literature but actually in action', writes Cornelius Ernst OP.[4] The Eucharist is pre-eminently the place where we enter into the reality of angelic mediation and ministry. Angels come into the visible world in order to take it into the invisible; they transform the mundane into the heavenly, and they do so in order that God may be known and be properly praised. The Eucharist is such an act of transformation, in its every part, and the liturgy gives full acknowledgement to the angels' part in it. We are joining in their ceaseless worship of God, which by Judaeo-Christian tradition is the very mode of angelic being, the tradition finding its origin in the vision of Isaiah, and its Christian focus in Revelation, where the song of the seraphim is sung ceaselessly, 'day and night' (Rev. 4:8).

The song 'Holy, Holy, Holy, is the Lord . . .', in Hebrew '*Qadosh, Qadosh, Qadosh, Adonai . . .*', is sung in Jewish worship, and has been given a key place in Christian liturgy. The *Sanctus*, or *Trishagion*, our most solemn proclamation of the holiness and glory of God, is firstly the angels' song, and the writer of this part of Isaiah probably intended them to be seen as the 'highest' angels; their voices shake the foundations of the thresholds. We might say their voices *are* the foundations of the thresholds, vibrating in pure praise of God. Worship of God must be the highest purpose of the angels, and they bring the whole of creation, and especially humankind, into that single activity, the only activity that is ultimately worthwhile. So an angel at its highest and purest is nothing but praise. Christian monastic life aims to imitate the angels in this; constant prayer punctuated by psalmody – *opus Dei*, the work of God – this was often described as an angelic vocation.[5] But every single person is called to follow a path that leads finally, in eternity, to 'nothing but praise', in a mode we cannot yet conceive. We can begin by recognizing the liturgy, together with our own prayer, to be the best way to make progress. The *Te Deum*, an early Latin hymn, first used in the monastic office for Sundays and festivals, places the community with the angels:

We praise you, O God; we acclaim you as the Lord.
Everlasting Father, all the world bows down before you.
All the angels sing your praise, the hosts of
heaven and all the angelic powers,
all the cherubim and seraphim call out to you in
unending song;
Holy, Holy, Holy, is the Lord God . . .[6]

In the Eucharistic Liturgy, after the penitential rite when the angels' prayers for us are requested, the *Gloria* is sung. This hymn, which opens with the acclamation of the multitude of angels above the fields of Bethlehem after Christ's birth had been announced to the shepherds, was first introduced into the liturgy before the fifth century. At first it was only for the first Mass of Christmas, before dawn, but Pope Symmachus (498–514) extended its use to Masses of Sundays and some feasts. At that time it was still sung in Greek; the earliest Latin form is found in the Gregorian Sacramentary (early seventh-century). The words of the angels' song from Luke form an introduction to the hymn; the next part is praise of God, followed by an invocation of Christ. With the angels and shepherds we proclaim the identity of the child in the manger whose sacrifice on the cross we celebrate. By singing the song of the angels we are present with them at these deeply significant events, in which they took part, and which they continue to proclaim in communal song with us. The *Gloria* is fittingly placed at the beginning of the Eucharist, recalling the beginning of Christ's human life and the initiation of his saving mission, which we are in the act of recalling, step by step.

Because the glorification of God in the salvation of mankind was not 'achieved' in its fullness until the sacrifice of Christ's passion, and even then its fruits had still to ripen, and to continue to ripen till the end of time, it is correct to view the angelic song as proclaiming not the work that had already been completed, but the plan and purpose that was yet to be done step by step: May God be given glory in the highest and may men in His grace find peace! *Gloria sit in excelsis Deo.* And if this were true of the song when the angels sang it, it is truer still when we on earth repeat it. Every day that the Church lives, every time the Church gathers her children in prayer, and particularly when she assembles them for the Eucharist, a new light flashes across the world, and the Church beholds, with mingled joy and longing, the approach of the kingdom of God, the advent, in spite of every obstacle, of the consummation of the great plan; that glory will come to God, and to mankind, peace and salvation.[7]

After the Liturgy of the Word, the preface to the central part of the Eucharist declares the fact of our joining with the angels' worship. The opening lines of the Preface state the end and means of all Christian worship:

Father, all-powerful and ever-living God, we do well (*vere dignum et justum est*) always and everywhere to give you thanks through Jesus Christ our Lord . . .

It is only through Christ that we and the angels can give God due praise. This is emphasized in nearly all the different forms of Preface used now. In some we ask to join with angels; 'May our voices be one with theirs' (Preface of Sundays III) as in the old Latin *Prefatio Communis*, after the named 'ranks' of angels; *cum quibus et nostras voces ut admitti jubeas, deprecamur, supplici confessione dicentes . . .* In the Eastern Orthodox Liturgy the congregation sees itself as not only joining in with the angels, but actually representing them, at the approaching solemn moment of consecration, by singing their scriptural hymn:

We who mystically represent the Cherubim, sing the thrice-holy hymn to the life-giving Trinity. Let us put away all worldly care, so that we may receive the King of All, invisibly escorted by the angelic hosts.[8]

The cherubim, who supported the ark of the covenant, are represented in the book of Revelation by the four living creatures who surround the throne of God. The four creatures of Ezekiel's vision are also called cherubim by him. The Orthodox Liturgy takes those present right into the awe-inspiring mystery of these great visions of the majesty of God. The western Church has suffered a reduction of the sublime visionary aspects of worship, but has gained, nevertheless, in a sense of the personal nearness and humility of Christ in the sacrament. The moment of preparation before the *Sanctus* should however be profoundly solemn, and the language of the Prefaces induce stillness and attention before we chant the 'thrice-holy hymn' of the angels, with them. All liturgies now add to Isaiah's text: '*Heaven* and earth are full of your glory'; at the coming of Christ heaven and earth are finally united, as here proclaimed by the union of human and angelic praise of God. For Christians the glory of God is concentrated in the body of the risen Christ, and we are reminded of this by the next part of the hymn:

Hosanna in the highest.
Blessed is he who comes in the name of the Lord.
Hosanna in the highest.

These are the songs of Jesus' disciples as they accompanied him on his entry into Jerusalem; his triumphant figure was carried, paradoxically, by a common colt. In the Eucharist we are celebrating, his majesty will be carried in ordinary bread and wine.

After the consecration of these earthly things, the priest may pray:

Almighty God, we pray that your angel may take this sacrifice to your altar in heaven . . .

Manoah and Gideon each recognize the true nature of their visitant when the angel ascends in the sacrificial fire, signifying God's acceptance of their offerings. It is our human action that we request be made acceptable to God, by the action of his angel. Thomas Aquinas notes that we ask that the angel may bear to the altar in heaven not the body of Christ, which abides there, but the oblation which we make of it in our prayer upon the earthly altar.[9] Because Christ, our mediator, descended, bringing God to humankind; because he died, rose again and ascended to heaven accompanied by his angels, we are instructed to offer

179

continually his perfect sacrifice in which humankind is brought to God. Therefore we first request the action of the Holy Spirit to come down upon our offerings and sanctify them (the *epiklesis*, or 'calling down'). All mediation and figurative movement in time and space cease in the consecration of the bread and wine which then is the risen body of Christ. Angelic action is stilled, time does not exist, as the material elements of our offering become uniquely divine. Then we pray that a mediating angel may raise our uplifted hands and hearts into heaven, a sort of *epiklesis* in reverse:

> Without doubt there is some participation of the angelic world in our oblation. But that can no longer be surprising after the *Sanctus* has been sung by heaven and earth conjointly. It is also in accord with the solidarity of the Christian order of salvation that the angels should in some way take part in the sacrifice of redemption.[10]

The ministry of angels is clearly seen here as also a form of humility, for their mediation ever assists human beings to be raised above them. The Bible tells us that angels rejoice over humanity's salvation. All that we understand by the word 'joy' can be related to the being of angels, i.e. a movement of the (human) spirit that lifts it towards its highest potential. 'I tell you,' said Jesus, 'there is open joy in the angels of God over one sinner who repents' (Luke 15:10).[11]

The ancient teaching of the Church is that the angels are at work in all its sacraments; fittingly, since in a sense angels are themselves sacramental, creatures by whom God transmits grace. There was a tradition that a 'type' of baptism is found in the story of the pool at Bethsaida, where some manuscripts of John's Gospel describe how an angel would go down into the water to activate it, after which the first person to enter would be healed of any sickness.[12] There were prayers in the old *ordo* of Extreme Unction, for Michael and the holy angels of God to come and lead the soul onwards into the Kingdom. The 'Final Commendation and Farewell' of a Requiem Mass makes a similar request.

In our familiarity with the liturgy we recognize the ministry of angels in the Church's worship, and our sharing in their continuous song of praise. Dante has an image which vividly illustrates the ceaseless activity of angelic ministry, both in this work of glorifying God, and in their labours in our service:

> In forma dunque di candida rosa
> mi si mostrava la milizia santa,
> che nel suo sangue Cristo fece sposa;
>
> ma l'altra, che volando vede e canta
> la gloria di colui che la innamora
> e la bontà che la fece cotanta,
>
> sì come schiera d'api, che s'infiora
> una fiata ed una si ritorna
> là dove suo lavoro s'insapora,
>
> nel gran fior discendeva, che s'adorna
> di tante foglie, e quindi risaliva
> là dove il suo amor sempre soggiorna.

(There was shown to me in the form of a white rose the holy army (the Church) which with his blood Christ made his bride; but the other army (the angels), who as they fly, see and sing the glory of him who arouses their love and the goodness which made them so great, are like a swarm of bees which at one moment dip into the flowers, and at another return to where their work is turned into honey. This host descended into the great flower which is adorned with so many petals and thence reascended to where its love abides for ever.)[13]

Notes for Part III Chapter 4

1   John Milton, *Arcades*, lines 72–3.
2   Walter Hilton, *Of Angels' Song*, from the Middle English.
3   T. S. Eliot, *Ash Wednesday*.
4   Cornelius Ernst, OP, 'How to see an angel', in *Multiple Echo, Explorations in Theology*, eds., F. Kerr OP and T. Radcliffe OP (Darton Longman and Todd, London, 1979) p. 194.
5   The religious life was also referred to as angelic because of the professed virginity of those in vows; they 'neither marry nor are given in marriage, but are like the angels in heaven' (Matt. 22:30).
6   The Liturgy of the Hours, 1971.
7   J. A. Jungmann, *The Mass of the Roman Rite* (Burns and Oates, London, 1959) p. 235.
8   The Divine Liturgy of St. John Chrysostom.
9   *Summa Theologica* III, 83.4 ad 9.
10 Jungmann, op.cit. p. 47.
11 This is my translation of *enopion* which can mean 'before the face of' or 'openly'. I feel the latter is a better expression of what Jesus was saying.
12 Erik Peterson, *The Angels and the Liturgy*, p. 31.
13 Dante, *Paradiso*, XXXI, 1–12, trans. D. B. Smith.

PART IV

Visions of the End

As I looked, thrones were placed, and one that was Ancient of Days took his seat; his raiment was white as snow, and the hair of his head like pure wool; his throne was fiery flames, its wheels were burning fire. A stream of fire issued and came forth from before him; a thousand thousand served him, and ten thousand times ten thousand stood before him.

(Dan. 7:9–10)

1. Apocalyptic Vision

'What,' it will be question'd, 'when the sun rises do you not see a
round disk of fire somewhat like a Guinea?' O no, no, no, I see an
Innumerable company of the Heavenly Host crying 'Holy, Holy, Holy
is the Lord God Almighty. I question not my Corporeal or Vegetative
eye any more than I would question a Window concerning a sight. I
look thro' it and not with it.

(WILLIAM BLAKE)

This book has so far dealt mostly with angels who have tasks to fulfil in the service of God, for particular people. The final section presents angels whose appearances convey meanings which are often not clear or easy to decipher. The angels are part of complex visions given to one person, for the benefit of many others. The visions point beyond the angels, bearing a significance that the seer must attempt to interpret.

Blake, the visionary, saw through his visions to God. In the above quotation he describes how he saw heaven in an earthly phenomenon. He also had sight of things that were not visible to other people; but although galaxies of visionary beings passed before him he did not stay with them; he saw beyond them, knowing his visions to be manifestations of divine glory. Earlier in the same text Blake wrote: 'It is not because Angels are Holier than Men or Devils that makes them Angels [sic], but because they do not expect holiness from one another, but from God only.'[1] Angels, like the moon, do not shine with their own light, and those who see them are aware of the greater light they reflect.

The prophet or visionary will see in all creation a manifestation of the Creator, as Blake exclaimed upon seeing the sun. The Psalmist sang: 'The heavens are telling the glory of God' (Ps. 19:1). But there is a special kind of vision given to only a few, of whom Blake is a post-Biblical example. More

185

than simply perceiving God's holiness revealed in his creation, Blake actually saw the heavenly host. He had a great many strange visions which he wrote about at length, and portrayed in his paintings and drawings. He could be said to be one of those foreseen by the prophet Joel to whom God said:

> It shall come to pass afterward that I will pour out my spirit on all flesh; your sons and your daughters shall prophesy, your old men shall dream dreams, and your young men shall see visions. Even upon the menservants and maidservants in those days I will pour out my spirit. (Joel 2:28–9)

The concrete phenomena of visions are very much in keeping with the character of Christianity. Christianity is a revealed and sacramental religion, and the Incarnation its greatest revelation of all. The incarnate Christ is the sacrament of God's saving presence with us, the ultimate sign, for he alone is both the sign and what is signified. But signs and visions may both reveal and conceal the truth, and Jesus is no exception. He is both man and God; the Godhead is hidden in the man. Similarly, in the sacrament of the Eucharist the God-man is concealed. There he is both the provider and the bread, the offerant and the offering. All other visions and revelations of God are distinct from God himself; our understanding of them must move on from the matter to the meaning. In Christ we stay, for in seeing him we see the Father. With him as the first and last divine revelation we need not be afraid of the many revelations and visions he has given to his prophets and people. Angels have frequently delivered the revelations and appeared in them in various forms, audible and visible.

Caution

There is, however, always the danger of false visions, as there is of false prophecy: 'And the Lord said to me, "The prophets are prophesying lies in my name . . ."' (Jer. 14:14) The Holy Spirit is the inspiration of all true prophecy, the giver of true visions. 'When the Spirit of truth comes, he will guide you into all truth,' said Jesus (John 16:13). But not all visions can be trusted; they may have their origins elsewhere than in the Holy Spirit. Paul warned against gullibility:

> there are false apostles, deceitful workmen, disguising themselves as apostles of Christ. And no wonder, for even Satan disguises himself as an angel of light. So it is not strange if his servants also disguise themselves as servants of righteousness. Their end will correspond to their deeds. (2 Cor. 11:13–15)

The surest measure of a vision's correspondence to truth is the end to which it leads. This may be revealed within the vision itself, or gradually unfolded in time. There is, however, no easy answer to the problem of discriminating between truth and illusion, between a vision or inspiration from God, or one from an evil source. (We have already discussed the role of adverse spirits acting under the authority of God.) The Church has always been aware of the need for careful discernment. For instance, in his *Spiritual Exercises* Ignatius of Loyola devotes some time to the problem, as it may emerge in individual cases. He suggests that a touchstone can be found in the personal disposition of the recipient of angelic inspiration.

> In the case of those who are making progress from good to better, the good angel touches such a soul sweetly, lightly, and gently, as a drop of water enters a sponge; and the evil angel touches it sharply and with noise and disturbance, as when a drop of water falls upon a rock. In the case of those who go from bad to worse, the said spirits touch it in a contrary manner; the reason of which difference is the disposition of the soul, according as it is contrary or similar to the aforementioned angels; for when it is contrary to them, they enter with noise and

sensible commotion, so that their coming may easily be perceived; but when it is similar to them, they enter in silence, as into their own house, by an open door.[2]

Confirmation of this theory can be found in the Gospels: Jesus spoke of the ease with which evil spirits might return to the soul recently emptied of them if the disposition of that soul has not changed. The unclean spirit will go back to his 'own house' (Luke 11:24). We have commented on the stillness and quiet of the scene of the annunciation to Mary as described in Luke's Gospel. The angel Gabriel is 'at home' in the heart of Mary.

Gabriel's appearance to Mary brought her a personal message, that she would conceive a son by the Holy Spirit. The message was also a revelation of the eternal fulfilment of God's promises to his people.

> He will be great, and will be called the Son of the Most High; and the Lord God will give to him the throne of his father David and he will reign over the house of Jacob for ever; and of his kingdom there will be no end. (Luke 1:32–3)

Mary's acceptance of the task God gave her included acceptance of her prophetic role. She received an 'apocalypse' – a revelation – from God, which referred both to her own life and to eternity.

Apocalypses

In the Bible there are several books that describe 'apocalyptic' visions, where a prophet is given messages that reveal the working out of God's design for the human race. The messages bring together the vision of a final consummation with insights into present tribulations. They are visions of angels, like the other appearances of angels to Abraham, Hagar, Jacob, Gideon and others, but these are far more strange and elaborate, and the angels have completely different functions in them. The angels in these visions are very important; they connect different parts of the vision itself, as the prophet is taken through separate experiences, and they bring the signs that convey the ultimate meanings to him. The context of these visions is quite different from the earlier stories; nevertheless they contain all the elements of angelic visitation that we have considered, and in which the nature of angels is shown forth. The recipients of the visions are standing on new ground; in the vision they may be taken over another threshold into the realm of the vision itself, without losing their human status. Some of the visionary creatures are monstrous, others have the appearance of people, with supernatural faculties. Fire plays an important part in the visions, also wind and water, three mysterious elements of this world. There are conversations with the angel messengers who often act as interpreters to the vision. The essential purpose of the visions is to relate the end of time, or the ultimate climax of humanity's relation to God, to the experience of the prophet and his people. The visions tell of a unity of Divine intention even while appearing fantastically different from the normal way of things. By cutting across natural laws and defying their limitations the angels demonstrate the conjunction of earth and heaven. They lift the natural directly into the supernatural before the eyes of the prophet.

At the beginning of this book I have given the example of Elisha's servant Gehazi, who is enabled to see angels who are already present. They do not appear, on the hillside above Dothan, they simply become visible to Gehazi upon Elisha's prayer. When Daniel sees the throne of the Ancient of Days and the figure of the Son of Man he is given power to see an eternal reality; something which is, not something that is made to happen before him. The form of his vision passed, but in describing it for us he can offer us the reality, as it was revealed to him. Stephen was stoned to death for declaring that he could see this same reality. Those who stoned him were unable to understand its permanence, they thought Stephen was an imposter, claiming identification with a prophet from the past (Acts 7).

Future, present and past are united in visions. The true vision is for now *and* then; visions that reveal the end of the world are not glimpses into the future, but glimpses of the unity of eternity, for in God the beginning and the end are one. On the human level, the vision will be carried in forms that are intelligible to the present time, so there may be some confusion between signs which relate to events in time, and those which point beyond time to the eternal. The prophet can speak only in his own words, and he will see phenomena that relate to his own experience, both personal and from tradition. In Matthew 24 and Luke 21 Jesus speaks prophetically, but even his utterances are a mixture of signs relating to imminent historical events and to the heavenly realities of judgement and the kingdom of God to come.

Reading an account of a prophetic vision is to partake of it in the present moment. Interpretation of the vision is continuously renewed, because of its timelessness, and because it can always be related afresh in the light of history. We are living now in an age of transition. There is a great restlessness and desire for change in the world. 'It doesn't take a prophet or a visionary to recognise that Apocalypse is in the air,' writes Dom Cyprian Smith; 'the conviction that society and culture as we know it is drawing to an end, that time is running out.'[3] The great writers who recorded the apocalyptic visions of the Bible were shown that God has much to say about how his power will move creation to its consummation, and how violence and evil will work themselves out, burnt up in the fire of his love.

The apocalyptic writings of the Bible and of later Jewish scriptures draw on each other in the way of all literary traditions. I shall discuss the visions of Ezekiel, Zechariah the prophet, John on Patmos, and Daniel. There are many connections of language and imagery in the writings of these four prophets. The connections are frequently found where the angels are concerned, and some people may feel that apparent borrowings from a tradition of angelic phenomena weakens the credibility of the prophet's account. But, rather than lessening the impact of their message, the connections serve to bring together the timeless elements of the visions. We are not concerned so much with the factuality, or historical reliability of the writings, as with what can be learned from them about God, and particularly in these texts, about the end of time. If angels exist in both timelessness and time, then their figuring in a vision in time which is concerned with revealing God's sovereignty outside time must be fitting to their nature and ministry. The visions are full of angels; they are almost entirely angelic manifestations.

Because the apocalyptic writings in the Bible are perhaps more difficult to read and understand than some other texts, I shall, as it were, walk through them, hoping to offer some elucidation at the same time as pointing out the effectiveness of the angels' part, and how essential they are to the vision's impact and interpretation. The richness of the imagery is also something to be enjoyed for its own sake, and for its attempts to bring us nearer to the very majesty of God. Angels are inescapably part of any apocalypse. Christ said several times in the Gospels, speaking of the Parousia:

> 'When the Son of Man comes in his glory, and all the angels with him, then he will sit on his glorious throne.' (Matt. 25:31)[4]

Notes for IV Chapter 1

[1] William Blake, from 'A Catalogue of a Vision of the Last Judgement' (1810). G. Keynes ed., *Blake: Complete Writings* (O.U.P., Oxford, 1972) pp. 616 and 617.
[2] 'Rules for the Fuller Discernment of Spirits', VII from *The Spiritual Exercises of St Ignatius Loyola*. W. H. Longridge ed. (O.U.P., Oxford, 1922) p. 193.
[3] Cyprian Smith OSB, *The Way of Paradox* (Darton Longman and Todd, London, 1987) p. 2.
[4] See also Matt. 16:27; 24:31; Mark 8:38; Luke 9:26.

2. The Prophets Ezekiel and Zechariah

And we have the prophetic word made more sure. You will do well to
pay attention to this as to a lamp shining in a dark place, until the
day dawns and the morning star rises in your hearts. First of all you
must understand this, that no prophecy of scripture is a matter of
one's own interpretation, because no prophecy ever came by the
impulse of man, but men moved by the Holy Spirit spoke from God.

(2 PET. 1:19–21)

Ezekiel and Zechariah were both priests: Ezekiel at the time
of the exile, living with his kindred Jews not far from Babylon;
Zechariah about a hundred years later, during the restoration
of Jerusalem and the building of the second temple.

The call of Ezekiel to prophecy is in many ways similar
to the call of Isaiah in his vision of the throne of God. They
are numbered among the great prophets. Isaiah was already
a prophet when he had his great vision, and Ezekiel, too, is
prepared; his priestly office has made him conscious of the
majesty and holiness of God. However, neither of them is
ready for the full impact of the glory revealed to them; they
each fall to the ground, and an angel comes to them. Isaiah
is purified by fire, Ezekiel by the sound of a voice:

> And he said to me, 'Son of man, stand upon your feet and
> I will speak with you.' And when he spoke to me, the
> Spirit entered into me and set me upon my feet; and I
> heard him speaking to me. And he said to me, 'Son of
> man, I send you to the people of Israel . . .' (Ezek. 2:1–3)

In both cases there is emphasis on the contrast between the
holiness of heaven and the earthliness of the prophet. In spite

of his apparent sanctity before God and in the light of the angels the prophet is nothing in himself, and his prostration acknowledges this. The address 'son of man' to Ezekiel (repeated many times throughout his book) underlines his mortality, his place among a sinful people, his oneness with them in the extremity of exile and degradation. But God has chosen this 'son of man' to be his voice.

'I send you to them; and you shall say to them "Thus says the Lord God."' (2:4)

When Ezekiel receives his vision he is by the river Chebar. Like Jacob he is far from home, and in this first instance probably alone, having wandered away from his kinsfolk; he is in a new place, a river-bank boundary, a threshold. Here, through a vision of angels, Ezekiel is shown the Divine glory. He begins his account of all that happens to him by saying: 'The heavens were opened, and I saw visions of God' (1:1). The opening of the heavens initiates a new opening of Ezekiel's understanding. He is taken into the great arena of angelic activity; his apocalyptic vision reveals the transcendence of God attended by his angels.

When the heavens open Ezekiel is aware of something rather like a tornado in the distance. As it approaches he can see a surrounding brilliance, and flashes from within which merge to appear as a flaming centre, its heart glowing. He begins to distinguish the forms of four creatures, angels, whose movement seems to empower the whole spectacle. He calls them 'living' creatures, using the same Hebrew word that occurs in Genesis for the breath of life. A similar connotation will emerge in another of Ezekiel's visions, accentuating that angels are signs of life. Perhaps Ezekiel here wishes to emphasize the vitality of the entire vision and of the four angels, who bear resemblance to the static 'kerubim', those composite figures who guard doorways and support thrones. Ezekiel's creatures have straight legs, with cloven hooves; each has four wings, and four faces: that of a man at the front, an eagle at the back, an ox and a lion on

193

either side. Under their wings they have human hands. 'And their wings, were spread out above; each creature had two wings each of which touched the wing of another, while two covered their bodies' (1:11). Later Ezekiel does call them the cherubim; doubtless they are in some ways living representatives of the creatures which supported the original throne of mercy, described in Exodus 25. These are anything but static however, and it is their movements that Ezekiel finds most hard to describe.

> And each went straight forward; wherever the spirit would go, they went, without turning as they went. In the midst of the living creatures there was something that looked like burning coals of fire, like torches moving to and fro among the living creatures; and the fire was bright, and out of the fire went forth lightning. And the living creatures darted to and fro, like a flash of lightning. (1:12–14)

The constant activity of angels is wonderfully displayed. Flickering fire and brightness are Ezekiel's chief impressions as the vision approaches him. It comes close enough for him to distinguish the details of the angels' appearance and then the 'chariot' touches the earth. Ezekiel makes out four wheels, each within a wheel, beside the angels. The wheels themselves are animate, having rims 'full of eyes'. The vehicle's movement is unlike any ordinary chariot:

> When they went, they went in any of their four directions without turning as they went . . . And when the living creatures went, the wheels went beside them; and when the living creatures rose from the earth, the wheels rose. Wherever the spirit would go, they went, and the wheels rose along with them; for the spirit of the living creatures was in the wheels. (1:17, 19–20)

When Ezekiel raises his eyes above the dance of the angelic chariot he sees the likeness of a firmament of crystal overhead; the angels' wings below move with 'the sound of many waters, like the thunder of the Almighty, a sound of tumult like the sound of a host.' Then comes a voice from above the firmament. At that the angels are still; 'they let down their wings'. The sudden stillness has as much power as all the previous movement. Above the firmament Ezekiel's gaze is held by what looks like a throne; seated on it is the form of a man, blazing with fire, surrounded by a great rainbow. The prophet falls to the ground.

Ezekiel describes what he sees as 'the appearance of the likeness of the glory of the Lord' (v. 28). The phrase 'the glory of the Lord', *kabod Yahweh* in Hebrew, is used in the Old Testament for the actual presence of God. While they knew that God was everywhere, the Jews understood a sacramental, or close, presence of Almighty God which was unspeakably awe-inspiring. His 'glory', *kabod*, came down on Sinai when Moses was given the law, and it dwelt, most directly, in the ark of the covenant which had been brought by Solomon to the temple in Jerusalem. Ezekiel is with the exiled Jews, separated from this sacramental presence. The prophet sees a vision of God's glory coming to his exiled people. However, the messages that Ezekiel is instructed to pass on are of reproof and warning. The word *kabod* means 'to be heavy', and by extension, as a metaphor 'to be weighted with honours'; and when the vision departs from Ezekiel this first time, he feels the burden of his call.

As the glory of the Lord arose from its place I heard behind me the sound of a great earthquake; it was the sound of the wings of the living creatures as they touched one another, and the sound of the wheels beside them, that sounded like a great earthquake. The spirit lifted me up and took me away, and I went in bitterness in the heat of my spirit, the hand of the Lord being strong upon me. (3:12–14)

Ezekiel is not left alone in his task. The spirit, or angel, sets him down with his people, and will return again. Ezekiel, like the Christ he does not yet know, must dwell among them, carrying the weight of the glory he has seen. After seven days the voice speaks to him again: 'Son of man, I have made you a watchman for the house of Israel' (v. 16). The prophet's role is like that of the angels; the eyes on the wheels of the chariot represent their unceasing watch. Then the 'glory of the Lord', the angelic chariot, appears again to Ezekiel's sight, and he understands that God is present here, in the midst of exiled Israel.

Angels at work in the visions

The sign of glory, the four cherubim with the sapphire throne above, appears four times to Ezekiel. Before the third appearance Ezekiel describes the angel who lifts him bodily and transports him, this time to Jerusalem:

> Then I beheld, and lo, a form that had the appearance of a man; below what appeared to be his loins it was fire, and above his loins it was like the appearance of brightness, like gleaming bronze. He put forth the form of a hand, and took me by a lock of my head; and the spirit lifted me up between earth and heaven, and brought me in visions of God to Jerusalem. (8:2–3)

There he sees a vision of the chariot again, by a gateway of the outer temple courts. The angel then takes him around the temple courts revealing hidden places where people are committing idolatry and sin. After this Ezekiel sees six destroying angels, in the form of men, each 'with his weapon for slaughter in his hand'. With them is another angel, 'a man clothed in linen with a writing case at his side'. They all stand beside the bronze altar in the temple. Ezekiel describes how the 'glory of the Lord' has left the chariot and rests on the threshold of the house. He hears the Lord command the seventh angel to mark out those who abhor the sinfulness all around them. The same thing occurs inthe book of Revelation; we see the action of an angel transmitting the

Divine righteousness in all its majesty and power to save. The angel who has this task in *Ezekiel* is instructed to mark on the foreheads of God's servants the Hebrew letter *tau*, then very similar to the sign of the cross. The destroying angels go through the city after him, slaughtering all those not so marked (9:1–7). Ezekiel cries out, 'Ah, Lord God, wilt thou destroy all that remains of Israel?'

The man clothed in linen is commanded to fetch purifying fire, recalling Isaiah's purging by a live coal from the heavenly altar. Here the fire comes from beneath the chariot:

'Go in among the whirling wheels underneath the cherubim; fill your hands with burning coals from between the cherubim, and scatter them over the city' . . . And he went in and stood beside a wheel, and a cherub stretched forth his hand from between the cherubim to the fire that was between the cherubim, and took some of it, and put it into the hands of the man clothed in linen who took it and went out. (10:2, 6–7)

The fire will cleanse the city itself, for the time when the exiles will return. Ezekiel watches the chariot rise up, with the *kabod Yahweh* above it, as he had seen it by the river Chebar.

The prophet must deliver the oracles as he is instructed by God, so that Israel 'shall know that I am the Lord'. Ezekiel has to make many prophecies of judgement, but amongst these are messages of hope and restoration. The promises of deliverance do not wait upon the repentance of the rebels; they come from God's unfailing love, his gratuitous covenant.

After some time Ezekiel has another vision, of a very different nature; he is taken by 'the spirit' and led around a valley full of dry bones, 'and lo, they were very dry'. The voice of God says:

'Prophesy to these bones and say to them, "O dry bones, hear the word of the Lord"' . . . So I prophesied as I was commanded; and as I prophesied there was a noise, and behold a rattling; and the bones came together, bone to its bone. And as I looked, there were sinews on them, and flesh had come upon them, and skin had covered them; but there was no breath in them. Then he said to me, 'Prophesy to the breath, prophesy, son of man, and say to the breath, "Thus says the Lord God: Come from the four winds, O breath, and breathe upon these slain, that they may live."' So I prophesied as he commanded me, and the breath came into them and they lived, and stood upon their feet, an exceedingly great host. (37:4 and 7–10)

In the valley Ezekiel actually takes part in the vision, and by it he learns what it means to be a prophet. It is to mediate the very life of God. Here we find the parallel from the book of Genesis: 'The Lord God formed man of dust from the ground, and breathed into his nostrils the breath of life; and man became a living being' (Gen. 2:7). Ezekiel is told to say to the 'breath' or spirit of life, 'Come from the four winds, O breath . . .' The mystery of the four winds, blowing from north, south, east and west, always moving across the face of the earth, finds expression in numerous images from all cultures.[1] In Zechariah we shall see angels identified as the four winds; in Revelation there are four angels 'standing at the four corners of the earth, holding back the four winds of the earth'; an angelic power is restrained by greater angels until the time is right (Revelation 7:1). Christ said his angels will gather his chosen 'from the four winds' (Matt. 24:31). Ezekiel's prophetic voice summons these symbolic spirits, and in the vision life is given to the bones. There will be new life, through the power of God in his angels, for the exiles, and for all people, whose home is in God:

'And you shall know that I am the Lord when I open your graves, and raise you from your graves, O my people. And I will put my Spirit within you, and you shall live, and I will place you in your own land; then you shall know that I, the Lord, have spoken, and I have done it, says the Lord.' (Ezek. 37:13–14)

Eventually Ezekiel is taken again in a vision to Jerusalem, where he is shown a new temple; an angel goes through every detail of its construction. Once again the angel has the appearance of a man 'of bronze'; he has a measuring line in his hand with which he makes precise measurements of every part of this new temple of God. When they get to the gate facing east, Ezekiel once more sees the *kabod Jahweh*, this time coming from the east, a sign of hope. 'And the sound of his coming was like the sound of many waters' (43:2). Ezekiel falls to the ground again. The spirit lifts him up, and takes him into the inner court of the temple, 'and behold, the glory of the Lord filled the temple.' (Isaiah, too, describes God as 'filling' the temple with his train, or 'the skirts of his robe' in the Hebrew.) God returns to his sanctuary, giving Ezekiel a sign that the Israelites will one day be able to worship in a truly holy place, their temple will be restored, and their rites accepted. The greatest sign of all is given by the angel when he takes Ezekiel back to the door of the temple, to show him a river of water flowing from below the threshold. This is 'living water', the same that is promised by God in his Son; the sign of God's life-giving power, the sign of the Holy Spirit. The angel takes Ezekiel deeper and deeper into this flowing water; 'it was a river that I could not pass through, for the water had risen; it was deep enough to swim in, a river that could not be passed through' (47:5). The river will give life to the driest of dry plains, make abundantly fruitful the most sterile of lakes. The eternal promise of this gift of life in the image of a river is well expressed by Ann Griffiths, an eighteenth-century Welsh mystic and visionary, in one of her hymns:

> Abundant freedom of entrance, for ever,
> into the dwelling place of the Three-in-One,
> water to swim in, not to pass through,
> Man as God and God as man.

> *(Mynediad helaeth byth i bara*
> *I fewn trigfannau tri'n un*

Dŵr i'w nofio heb fynd trwyddo
Dyn yn Dduw, a Duw 'n ddyn.)[2]

True prophets are true to their vision. They do not allow their lack of understanding to inhibit them. We who have not seen what they see have only their words to go on; the prophet must write, as John was instructed on Patmos:

> The revelation of Jesus Christ . . . made known by sending his angel to his servant John who bore witness to the word of God . . . I heard behind me a loud voice, like a trumpet saying, 'Write what you see in a book . . .'
> (Revelation 1:1–2 and 10–11)

How difficult it is for these visionaries to describe what they saw! For the reader, there may be debate as to whether the prophet is a great allegorist, a fabulist, who can produce images to shape the message he feels inspired to pass on; or is he truly an impartial recipient of images he then records with accuracy? He can be both of these, and more than both. Prophet and poet have much in common; the prophets whose words we read in the Bible have the gift of poetic discourse. It is the only mode in which their visions can be recorded and their prophecies delivered. The 'poems' that attempt to describe the visions give the impression that the visions are not clear-cut or sequential; they are not played like a video before the prophet, but flash and move and change in the manner of our most unlikely dreams. Sometimes the seer is on the stage of the vision, sometimes it lights up above him; voices come from behind him or far away; sounds are over-whelmingly loud, or distant, and almost impossible to put into words. Ezekiel strains to express the brilliance and fantasy of his vision: 'it was like . . . they had the likeness of . . . the appearance of . . . a sound like . . .' Comparisons can never come up to what he sees, or thinks he sees. For the whole thing must surely be so far beyond his comprehension that he can but gaze on it, stammering, 'What is this? Am I dreaming? Where is it – here? there? . . .' For Ezekiel the only

200

thing is to fall to the ground and wait on God; to obey the deep religious instinct which is the fundamental characteristic of every prophet. This is where the greatness of these great prophets lies. They know how to empty themselves and be filled with the Holy Spirit. Then they know that what they see and hear is reality of the highest order. Later they sit down to write the 'poem' that attempts to express it all as truly as possible.

In the final chapter of Ezekiel the prophet himself fades from the scene; the last words of the book are: 'The Lord is there.' This is the ultimate meaning of all the visions, and the angels' role throughout is to lead the prophet, and those who receive his account, to this understanding. God is revealing through signs presented by his angels that divine power and majesty will triumph over every evil, in the final consummation. The angels in Ezekiel are themselves creatures of splendour and mystery, conveying the glory of God, in more senses than one. Some are pitilessly destructive of evil, but the guiding angel brings Ezekiel to the symbolic living water, the overflowing mercy of God that will pour from Christ's side on the cross. There will be room for all the tribes in the new temple, the one seen by John in his Revelation, and as the angel says to Ezekiel:

'The Lord is there.'

Zechariah

The angels of the visions are at God's command; like the messenger angels they represent God. The prophet Zechariah proclaims this fact, after he has seen his apocalyptic visions:

The Lord will appear over them, and his arrow go forth like lightning; the Lord God will sound the trumpet, and march forth in the whirlwinds. (Zech. 9:14)

All that the angels perform in the visions are the actions of God; the visions are signs of his omnipotence.

201

'I saw in the night,' writes Zechariah. He records a sequence of eight visions through which, like Ezekiel, he is guided by an angel-interpreter. The series begins with the sight of four horsemen with coloured steeds:

> I saw in the night, and behold, a man riding upon a red horse! He was standing among the myrtle trees in the glen; and behind him were red, sorrel and white horses. Then I said, 'What are these, my lord?' The angel who talked with me said to me, 'I will show you what they are.' So the man who was standing among the myrtle trees answered, 'These are they whom the Lord has sent to patrol the earth.' And they answered the angel of the Lord who was standing among the myrtle trees, 'We have patrolled the earth . . .' (1:8–11)

Here again are the angel-watchers, the eyes in the wheels of Ezekiel's vision, and we are reminded also of Satan the adversary and the other angels who, in the book of Job, were roaming the earth. The patrollers in Zechariah have come to report that the world is 'at rest', but it is not a good rest, for there is only one true rest, God himself. This is explained to Zechariah by the angel who talks with him. This angel acts as interpreter to all eight visions, and to begin with he tells Zechariah that the Lord says, 'I am very angry with the nations that are at ease; for while I was angry but a little they furthered the disaster. Therefore . . . I have returned to Jerusalem with compassion; my house shall be built in it' (vv. 15–16).

The eight visions

As the visions unfold, it is evident that not all the figures seen by Zechariah are angels. We can distinguish the angels, who are at work in bringing the visions before Zechariah and in interpreting them, from the phenomena of the visions that are purely symbolic, with no life of their own. The second vision is a sight of four horns, which signify the enemies of Israel. Horns are phallic symbols and are recurring images of aggression in the Old Testament. Four smiths appear to 'terrify and scatter' the horns. In the third vision a man with a measuring line is seen; he represents a worldly way of thinking. He is not like the angel with the measuring line who conducts Ezekiel through the visions of the temple. Zechariah asks the man where he is going, and he replies, 'To measure Jerusalem, to see what is its breadth and what is its length.' At once Zechariah's angel comes forward; another angel meets him and is told, 'Run, say to that young man, "Jerusalem shall be inhabited as a village without walls, because of the multitude of men and cattle in it."' There is to be no circumscribing the city of the people of God. 'For I will be a wall of fire round about,' says the Lord, 'and I will be the glory within her. (2:1–5). We might compare Jesus' words to the woman at the well: 'The hour is coming when neither on this mountain nor in Jerusalem will you worship the Father. . . . The hour is coming, and now is, when true worshippers will worship the Father in spirit and in truth' (John 4:21 and 23). Zechariah's angel goes on to say:

> Sing and rejoice, O daughter of Zion, for lo, I come and I will dwell in the midst of you, says the Lord. And many nations shall join themselves to the Lord in that day, and shall be my people; and I will dwell in the midst of you . . . Be silent, all flesh, before the Lord, for he has roused himself from his holy dwelling. (2:10–11 and 13)

Zechariah is then shown the trial scene of the Jewish high priest (described in chapter 3, Part I above), which proclaims that the temple worship shall be purified. After this Zechariah is awakened by his angel; that is to say, his eyes are opened like Gehazi's to see the next vision. He is shown a golden lampstand with seven lamps, flanked by two olive trees. Oil, fire and light are symbols of sanctity and watchfulness; signifying a new era of true worship. The angel quotes the word of the Lord: '"Not by might, nor by power, but by my spirit," says the Lord of hosts' (4:6). Zechariah is told that the seven lamps represent 'the eyes of the Lord, which range through the whole earth'; the ever-watchful angels of God. The oil is the oil of anointing, sign of the Holy Spirit. The olive trees are 'the two anointed who stand by the Lord of the whole earth' (4:14). The text is left open to interpretation; we might now see in it a Trinitarian symbol. The 'two witnesses' of Revelation 11:3 are similarly mysterious figures, who undoubtedly relate to this vision of Zechariah; they are described as 'the two olive trees and the two lampstands which stand before the Lord.' Their destiny, as seen by John, may form a paradigm of Christ who is more than once referred to as 'witness' in John's book.

In Zechariah's seventh vision there appears a container, called an ephah, where sits Israel's guilt in the form of a woman. Two winged women lift the ephah, removing it to the land of wickedness, Babylonia. None of these are characteristically angelic figures; they simply present an allegorical scenario.

Zechariah's eighth and final vision brings the four equestrian angels again, this time as four chariots with red, black, white and dappled horses respectively. They appear, riding from a pass between two mountains of bronze. The angel who talks with Zechariah tells him, 'These are the four spirits (or winds) of the heavens, which go forth from standing before the Lord of all the earth' (6:5). I have used the Authorized Version for this verse, since it is nearer to the Hebrew. Other translations have the chariots 'go forth to the four winds after presenting themselves to the Lord of all the earth.' These translators fail to identify the angels with their sign. Here Zechariah's vision proclaims, with the Psalmist, 'You make your angels winds, and your ministers a flaming fire.'[3] The horses are raring to go off, to the four corners of the world, and the angel says, 'Go, patrol the earth.' In the first vision the angelic horsemen are like figures in a painting, standing in a grove of myrtle trees; they have just returned from a journey. They finally appear as warlike or racing charioteers, impatient to be away again, carrying out the word of God. Zechariah can be assured that the things he has been shown in the intervening visions reveal the ongoing fulfilment of

God's promises. God marches forth in his whirlwinds, the angels who are 'the four winds'.

Zechariah has been accompanied through all the visions by his angel-interpreter. His last words to Zechariah are words of promise, and command:

> And those who are far off shall come and help to build the temple of the Lord; and you shall know that the Lord of hosts has sent me to you. And this shall come to pass, if you will diligently obey the voice of the Lord your God. (6:15)

The angel speaks with the voice of God; the angels of the vision have shown Zechariah how God sees the different aspects of the condition of Israel. The remaining chapters of Zechariah set out his oracles and prophecies of God's judgement and consolation, as he has learned them. These oracles announce God's demand for purer worship, obedience and trust. At the same time they give assurance of the Divine presence and power which will take the people through the trials of the world victoriously.

> And the Lord will become king over all the earth; on that day the Lord will be one, and his name one (14:9).

Notes for Part IV Chapter 2

[1] Aeolus, god of the winds in later Greek and Roman mythology, is depicted by Virgil as keeping the winds imprisoned in a cave where they race round furiously. With Juno's bribe they are released and sweep the earth with tornado blasts, nearly destroying Aeneas and the Trojans who have survived the war. (*Aeneid* 1:50f.)

[2] A. M. Allchin, *Ann Griffiths: The Furnace and the Fountain* (University of Wales Press, Cardiff, 1987) p. 16.

[3] See note 2 on pp. 135f., chapter 4, Part II.

3. Daniel

. . . For he is the living God, enduring for ever. His kingdom shall
never be destroyed and his dominion shall be to the end. He delivers
and rescues, he works signs and wonders, in heaven and on earth.

(DAN. 6:26–7)

The prophet Daniel received, as the climax of his apocalyptic vision, a sign of the parousia: 'one like a son of man' coming with the clouds of heaven. Because of this his book stands out among the other Old Testament apocalypses. Angels are important throughout the book, and carry its message into the New Testament, with the appearance of Gabriel who is first named here.

The story of Daniel, in its various stages, gives account of all the most significant roles of angels. We have discussed the angel rescuers of the story, as they save Daniel and his three companions from terrible deaths at the hands of the Babylonian kings. The prophet and his companions grow in strength and perception of God, until Daniel is ready to receive the gift of apocalyptic vision, interpreted for him by the angel Gabriel. Daniel is himself an interpreter; his status in the royal court has been achieved through his powers of insight into dreams and signs. However, Daniel finds his own visions hard to understand, owing to his genuine humility. He needs the assistance of Gabriel. The angel reveals a deepening personal relationship with Daniel, as the story progresses. The figure of Gabriel, guiding Daniel with great sensitivity, brings together the roles of guardian, messenger and interpreter into one. In Daniel the angel is unquestionably a 'person'.

The book has come to us as a collection of narratives in three different languages. Parts of it are considered by some to be secondary to the canon because they appear only in the Greek Septuagint; these are the prayer of Azariah and the hymn of the three young men in the furnace, and also the stories of Susannah, Bel, and the dragon. Apart from these, the opening verses of the book, and chapters 8 to 12, are in Hebrew, the rest in Aramaic. The chapters in Aramaic tell Daniel's story, and are written in the third person, except for chapter 7. The Hebrew chapters, in the first person, are more like the prophetic books of Ezekiel and Zechariah.

Visions in the night

First-person narrative begins in the second verse of chapter 7, where the account of Daniel's apocalyptic visions opens. Daniel says, 'I saw in my vision by night, and behold the four winds of heaven were stirring up the great sea.' The familiar 'four winds' set the vision in motion, and the prophet sees four monsters emerge from the sea. They symbolize the brutal nature of the empires that had been suppressing the Jews, but Daniel does not at once seek an interpretation; he is looking at a gathering of the court of heaven that unfolds before him. Visually and poetically Daniel's vision is the most clearly significant of all the Old Testament visions of heaven:

> Thrones were placed
> and one that was
> Ancient of Days took his seat;
> his raiment was white as snow, and the hair
> of his head like pure wool,
> his throne was fiery flames, its wheels were
> burning fire.
> A stream of fire issued and came forth from before him;
> a thousand thousand served him and ten
> thousand times ten thousand stood before
> him; the court sat in judgement, and the
> books were opened. (7:9–10)

The Aramaic phrase 'Ancient of Days' appears nowhere else in the Bible. His entry, and enthronement on the chariot of fire, bestow a sense of awe and pure reverence. His power is represented by the 'stream of fire', and around him Daniel sees the myriad angelic host. With solemnity the judgement is given and at once the four beasts are destroyed. Daniel's gaze returns above:

> and behold with the clouds of heaven
> there came one like a son of man,
> and he came to the Ancient of Days and was
> presented before him.
> And to him was given dominion and glory and
> kingdom, that all peoples, nations and
> languages should serve him; his dominion is
> an everlasting dominion, which shall not
> pass away, and his kingdom one that shall
> not be destroyed. (vv. 13–14)

The simplicity of the vision is striking. The term 'son of man', that Christ chose for himself, here in the Aramaic *bar enosh*, is fittingly applied to the figure that represents all humankind. The Aramaic word and its Hebrew equivalent are used generically in the Bible, and also to indicate someone specially chosen, such as a prophet. Daniel asks one of the attendant angels to explain the vision, and the angel tells him that the defeated monsters are kings of the earth, but that there is an eternal kingdom, and into this will come the 'saints of the Most High'. The figure like a son of man comes before the Ancient of Days in the name of the whole human race, who shall 'possess the kingdom for ever, for ever and ever' (v. 18).

The High Priest said to Jesus during his trial, 'Tell us if you are the Christ, the Son of God.' Jesus said to him, 'You have said so, and I tell you, hereafter you will see the Son of Man seated at the right hand of power, and coming on the clouds of heaven' (Matt. 26:63–4). The High Priest reacted violently to this; to him and the scribes and elders the claim was impossibly great. Had they but known, the Son of Man was actually standing before them; his dominion and its inheritance were being established in the very events they were living through, while at the same time having been established from before the beginning. Daniel's first angel-interpreter is quite impersonal; its final words to Daniel are 'Here is the end of the matter' (Dan. 7:28), which somehow befits the totality of the vision, particularly as we now see it with Christian hindsight. Daniel is shaken; he evidently feels there must be more to come, and like Mary, he muses over it all:

> As for me, Daniel, my thoughts greatly alarmed me, and my colour changed; but I kept the matter in my mind. (7:28)

Angels and the unfolding of history

Daniel's next vision is of a river; on the bank a ram and a he-goat do battle, symbolizing the warring Persian and Greek empires. Again Daniel cannot understand the vision, and at this point Gabriel makes his entry:

> And behold, there stood before me one having the appearance of a man. And I heard a man's voice between the banks of the [river] Ulai, and it called, 'Gabriel, make this man understand the vision.' (8:15–16)

For all his high authority, Gabriel is commanded by a mystery voice to give Daniel the interpretation; a servant of the servants of God, Gabriel the great messenger now addresses Daniel as 'son of man', *ben adam* in Hebrew. Daniel finds the proximity of the angel frightening; he loses consciousness. 'But he touched me, and set me on my feet' (v. 18). Gabriel has a gentle and courteous manner, even while his appearance is terrifyingly majestic and Daniel is completely overawed by him. He brings not only the word of God to Daniel, but also God's love for him. Like Zechariah, father of John the Baptist, Daniel is 'righteous before God'

209

and chosen for special revelations, and as with Zechariah, the great angel messenger next comes to Daniel while he is praying. Daniel is confessing his own sins and those of his people, and asking God to explain why Jeremiah's prophecy of the end of Jerusalem's desolation is not fulfilled. (Apart from once in the book of Revelation, this is the only place in the Bible where an angel is described as flying.)

> While I was speaking in prayer, the man Gabriel, whom I had seen in the vision at the first, came to me in swift flight at the time of the evening sacrifice. He came and he said to me, 'O Daniel, I have now come out to give you wisdom and understanding. At the beginning of your supplications a word went forth, and I have come to tell it to you, for you are greatly beloved; therefore consider the word, and understand the vision.' (9:21–3)

Daniel is saddened by Gabriel's following explanation that Israel is to suffer for seventy times seven years. He mourns ritually for three weeks. He is standing beside the river Tigris when Gabriel comes again, as a glorious figure not unlike the appearance of Christ to John on Patmos. The angel is sent to dispel Daniel's sadness by a blaze of light. Again Daniel loses consciousness. Gabriel touches him, saying, 'O Daniel, man greatly beloved . . .' (10:11). Daniel stands up, still trembling.

> Then he said to me, 'Fear not, Daniel, for from the first day that you set your mind to understand and humbled yourself before God, your words have been heard, and I have come because of your words.' (10:12)

Gabriel begins to tell Daniel that the angels are interacting in the salvation of God's people. This text is one of the points of reference for the tradition of the 'angels of the nations'. Gabriel has been fighting for Israel against the 'prince of the kingdom of Persia', and Michael, 'one of the chief princes', has taken over the campaign (10:13). The angels apparently contend with one another on behalf of their respective nations. In Jewish tradition the nations of the world are placed under the tutelage of angels, each nation having its own angelic patron. There are various strands in this tradition, which cannot be disentangled. An early text, the Song of Moses in Deuteronomy, has given rise to one strand:

> When the Most High divided the nations, when he separated the sons of Adam, he set the bounds of the nations according to the number of the angels of God. (Deut. 32:8, LXX)[1]

The notion became established that there were 'seventy' ministering angels who, with Michael at their head, were allotted the 'seventy' nations descended from the sons of Noah. The seventy angels were later known as the 'watchers' or 'shepherds' (Dan. 4:17 etc.).[2] Daniel's confidence is to be restored by the knowledge that human beings are not left abandoned on earth; God's princes are gloriously arrayed for their rescue. But Daniel's fear will not leave him, he is prostrate and speechless. Another angel touches his lips. What a contrast are these direct gentle touches with the talk of war and violence! Daniel says to this angel:

> 'O, my lord, by reason of the vision pains have come upon me, and I retain no strength. How can my lord's servant talk with my lord? For now no strength remains in me, and no breath is left in me.' Again one having the appearance of a man touched me and strengthened me. And he said, 'O man greatly beloved, fear not, peace be with you; be strong and of good courage.' And when he spoke to me I was strengthened and said, 'Let my lord speak, for you have strengthened me.' (10:16–19)

Gabriel speaks again, telling Daniel that he and Michael are fighting together for the defence of Israel (10:21). He gives, as a prophetic revelation to Daniel, a brief history of Hellenistic wars and the fall of the Persian empire. At the end of it Daniel looks back to the river and sees two angels, standing one on each side (12:5).

The river now seems to represent the threshold or boundary between earth and heaven, and angels stand one on either side. The angels in apocalyptic visions cross the boundary, coming to the prophets to guide their sight and understanding in order that they may see into heaven, where angels are revealing what will be. 'For the vision is for days yet to come' (Dan. 10:14). Daniel is deeply affected by all that he has been shown; he stands out as a man of reverence and sensitivity, matched in the story by the figure of Gabriel. Looking beyond the two angels and the river Daniel sees Gabriel, 'the man clothed in linen', above the waters of the stream. The sight can now be interpreted as a simplified re-enactment of the throne of God Daniel saw at first. Instead of a stream of fire, a river of living water flows from the great angel of God, flanked by angel ministers. Daniel is now calm; he asks the angel, 'How long shall it be till the end of these wonders?' The angel's response is to raise his arms to heaven.

> I heard him swear by him who lives for ever that it would be for a time, two times and half a time. (12:7)

Jesus said: 'Of that day and hour no one knows, not even the angels of heaven' (Matt. 24:36). These words of Jesus follow his own prophecy of tribulations in the world before the end of time. But he has the words of eternal life: 'Heaven and earth will pass away, but my words will not pass away.' Daniel, it would seem, has had a glimpse of the coming dominion of Christ when he brings the kingdom to the Father, and all humanity with him. Gabriel assures Daniel that he will see that final apocalypse:

> Go your way until the end; and you shall rest, and shall stand in your allotted place at the end of the days. (12:13)

Notes for Part IV Chapter 3

[1] I have quoted the Septuagint version of this text because it is clearly expressed; the Rabbis base their accepted reading on a conflation of texts, including this one. The concept of 'angels of the nations' has little interest for us nowadays, except as a piece of Jewish tradition. Protection against enemy nations was believed to be given by God to his chosen people, as the Old Testament frequently proclaims. Angels were assigned the task of fighting on behalf of the nations over whom they watched. These warring angels often fought amongst themselves, it appears; a Rabbinical prayer asked that God would bring peace to 'the household above', i.e. the angel princes, in order that there might be peace in the 'household below'. It seems that strife among the angel princes was bringing nations into conflict on earth. See G. Moore, *Judaism*, Vol. II (C.U.P., Cambridge, 1927) p. 242.

[2] Also the apocryphal book of Enoch, 1:5 etc. A 'watcher' or 'wakeful one' (Hebrew *ir*) appears in many forms in Jewish angelology.

4. John's Revelation

And he said to me, 'These words are trustworthy and true. And the Lord, the God of the spirits of the prophets, has sent his angel to show his servants what must soon take place. And behold, I am coming soon.'

(REV. 22:6–7)

Like Ezekiel, Zechariah and Daniel, John is in exile. He is on the island of Patmos, a no-man's land, a threshold place. It is the Lord's Day, the day that recalls Jesus' opening of the kingdom of heaven for all time (1:10). The great difference between John's revelation and those of the Old Testament prophets is, of course, the recognition of Christ. Christian believers will see him in all prophecy, and John is a prophet of the Christian age. (It is probable, but not certain, that it is not the same John as the evangelist, or the apostle.) Christ appears in his visions in many different forms; they all show the apocalyptic Christ, revealed by signs. Words are heard by the prophet, either as though spoken by Christ himself, or through an angel; at times it is hard to distinguish the transitions made within the text, as in the quotation at the head of this chapter. In John's apocalypse Christ figures as 'the angel of God's presence'[1] and in it we can see enacted by signs his relation to the angels; they are messengers of Christ who is both the message and the first messenger of God. Christ takes on several images in the course of the book, and I will comment firstly on these images since they are 'angelic' figures, and may be seen as culminations of all the angel-images that have gone before.

John's first vision of Christ is in glory, resembling the *kabod Yahweh* seen by Ezekiel. This figure is blazing with signs of celestial splendour; fire, gold, bronze, snowy-whiteness, a two-edged sword, his face like the sun, his voice

214

the sound of many waters (Rev. 1:12–16). He is standing amidst seven golden lamps (cf. Zechariah) and holding seven stars in his right hand. The stars, he explains, are seven angels, the guiding angels of the churches John is writing to (1:20); the whole book is a letter to the Christian Church of that time. This image implies that Christ always holds the angels in his hand; they can do nothing without him. The prophet is brought to understand that there is nevertheless a clear distinction between Christ and his angels. During his visions John hears Christ's words spoken to him as 'true words of God', and twice he falls at the feet of an angel spokesman to worship him. The angel at once says, 'You must not do that! I am a fellow-servant with you and your brethren who hold the testimony of Jesus. Worship God!' (19:10 and 22:9). It is unusual for an angel to align itself with humanity; their service is so much higher, it seems, than ours. Nevertheless, angels, prophets and ordinary people are all fellow-servants, *syndouloi*, serving God and each other. The greatest wonder is that God should have come among us as one who serves, in the person of Jesus Christ, who was for a time made lower than the angels, and here appears in angel-like images.

Christ appears under different signs

John receives Christ's messages for the seven churches, and after this he records, 'I looked, and lo, in heaven, an open door!' (4:1). John sees a throne surrounded by a rainbow, 'with one seated upon the throne'. It is 'He who lives for ever and ever'; John makes no attempt to describe him, but soon Christ appears again, under another sign: the Lamb, looking 'as though it had been slain'. It takes the sealed scroll from the right hand of the One on the throne. Only the Lamb is worthy to open the seals, and read the scroll (ch. 5). The scroll itself may be seen as another sign of Christ, the word of God. Both John and Ezekiel are asked to eat a scroll, a figuration of the Eucharist. As if to demonstrate the ubiquity of Christ and the contrasting nature of his signs, the figure summoned to appear, upon the Lamb's breaking the first seal, is a man riding a white horse: the crowned Conqueror (6:1–2). Later, Christ appears under a sixth sign, as the 'male child', rescued at birth from the dragon, and taken up to God and to his throne (12:5). In chapter 14 one comes, 'like a son of man' seated upon a cloud, as in Daniel's vision. He is again crowned, and now carries a sickle, with which he reaps the earth. This sign identifies Christ, the Son of Man, with his angel-reapers, whom, Jesus said, he will send out at the 'close of the age' to reap the harvest of good and evil (Matt. 13:39–43).

The next appearance is again as the rider of a white horse. Once more, John tells us, he sees 'heaven opened',

and behold, a white horse! He who sat upon it is called Faithful and True, and in righteousness he judges and makes war. His eyes are like a flame of fire, and on his head are many diadems; and he has a name inscribed which no one knows but himself. He is clad in a robe dipped in blood and the name by which he is called is The Word of God. (19:11–13)

This warrior Christ, 'King of kings and Lord of lords', rides at the head of the armies of heaven in a battle that defeats evil. The 'beast' and its false prophet are thrown into the lake of burning sulphur, and the rest of the 'kings of the earth' are 'slain by the sword of him who sits upon the horse, the sword that issues from his mouth' (19:21). If we react against this image of the Prince of peace, we must remember that John's vision reveals humanity's passage through war, bloodshed and horror into the reign of love. Finally, he says, 'I saw a new heaven and a new earth; for the first heaven and the first earth had passed away . . . And he who sat upon the throne said, "Behold, I make all things new." Also he said, "Write, for these words are trustworthy and true"' – the names given to the Word of God (21:1 and 5). When God speaks from the throne his very words are another image of Christ, the Word.

After hearing this promise John is taken by an angel to

see the new Jerusalem. 'And I saw no temple in the city, for its temple is the Lord God, the Almighty, and the Lamb' (21:22). Isaiah and Ezekiel knew this, when they said that the glory of the Lord 'filled the temple'; and now John, too, sees the river of the water of life flowing 'from the throne of God and the Lamb' (22:1). And then the angel's words become the promise of Jesus, that I quoted at the beginning, 'Behold, I am coming soon . . . I Jesus have sent my angel to you with this testimony for the churches . . .' (22:12 and 16). Earlier, John said, 'the testimony of Jesus is the spirit of prophecy' (19:10). This can mean that a true prophetic spirit witnesses to Jesus as the Son of God, but it also means, in a stronger sense, that the spirit of prophecy lies in Jesus' own testimony. His testimony is his very person, his obedience to the Father, and his passion and death. He is both the witness and the testimony. John's apocalypse begins and ends with a sign of Christ: the book concludes with the words 'Come, Lord Jesus'. The final image of Christ is the man, Jesus of Nazareth, who died on the cross, and rose again. It was the angels who said to the disciples, after Jesus had ascended, 'This Jesus, who was taken up from you into heaven, will come again in the same way as you saw him go into heaven' (Acts 1:11).

Angels act in the drama

These different Christ-images in John's Revelation must not be confused with the angels, whose roles are many and varied, but whose work is to present the signs of Christ. At his ascension angels delivered the promise of Jesus' return; here, angels deliver the drama of John's apocalypse. They act in this drama in different ways: as interpreters, as the bearers of revelation, and as participants. It can be helpful to see John's vision in terms of a play, provided these terms do not fix it in too rigid a structure, for it is as complicated and shifting as the dance of Ezekiel's chariot.[2] There are, however, four 'acts', all of which are based upon the mystical number seven. The first is the prologue and the writing of the seven letters to the churches, covering the first three chapters. 'Act 2' reveals the unsealing of the seven-sealed scroll (chs. 4–7); 'Act 3' the sounding of the seven trumpets (chs. 8–14); 'Act 4' the pouring out of seven plagues upon the earth, followed by the fall of Babylon. The climax is reached in chapter 21 with the vision of the new Jerusalem, and the last verses of the chapter form an epilogue. The angels who participate in this drama appear as individuals who perform specific tasks such as interpreting the vision, and as stylized groups: sevens, fours, the twenty-four elders, and the 'multitude of the heavenly host'.

Throughout his vision John is guided by angels who instruct and interpret. The first thing he hears is a voice commanding him to write. The angelic voice comes again after the seven letters to the churches have been dictated, and the first group of seven is the seven 'angels of the churches', the 'seven stars' in Christ's right hand. As we have discussed in the chapter on guardian angels, they may be seen as the 'kindred spirits' of the different churches; so the letters are addressed to the angels, not to the bishops or elders. The angels are responsible, in a way; they have in their hands the welfare of the churches. The messages are delivered from the 'angel' figure of Christ; the guardian angels are responsible to him. It is his voice they and the people must have ears to hear. After this, when heaven opens before the prophet's eyes, he hears his angel interpreter speak again. 'Come up hither, and I will show you what will take place after this' (4:1). We know that this angel is to be John's guide, though much of the time it is in the background. However, towards the end of the vision this guiding angel emerges more and more as a person. Now, with the angel-guide John looks on the vision of the throne surrounded by the twenty-four elders, with four living beasts, a reminder of Ezekiel's vision. John hears a great song of praise, and the voice of a mighty angel asking, 'Who is worthy to open the scroll and break its seals?' When John weeps to find no one worthy, one of the elders becomes an interpreter, saying to John;

'Weep not; lo, the Lion of the tribe of Judah, the root of David, has conquered, so that he can open the scroll and its seven seals. (5:5)

The Lion of Judah is the Lamb of God. One of the twenty-four, this dramatic and symbolic group of figures, is separated off to act as John's interpreter. The same happens after the 'sealing' of the faithful, in chapter 7, forming another link with the prophetic visions of Ezekiel who saw twenty-five men profaning the temple by turning from God to worship the rising sun. Soon after this Ezekiel was shown how the blasphemous would be slaughtered, but the faithful marked on their foreheads to save them from destruction (Ezek. 8 and 9). In John's vision the twenty-four elders continually praise God on his throne, showing how God is truly worshipped and served by his faithful angels, and how they rejoice at the salvation of the human race by the Lamb of God. The saved are represented by a great multitude, dressed in white.

And he said to me: 'These are they who have come out of the great tribulation; they have washed their robes and made them white in the blood of the Lamb. Therefore are they before the throne of God and serve him day and night within his temple . . . (7:14–15)

In the end, the angels and all God's people will be as one in his eternal presence.

After the opening of the scroll, the four beasts now have a task to perform; upon the opening of the first four seals by the Lamb they each cry 'Come!' to summon four riders (6:1–8). The first is Christ the conqueror on his white horse, the others are images of the evils he will conquer, war, famine, and death. These riders are allegorical figures rather than angels. Another group of four angels follows this 'scene'; they are the angels of the four winds. Here they stand for destruction, and are held in check by the voice of another powerful angel (7:1–3).

A great silence prepares for the seven 'angels of the presence', and the blowing of the trumpets. John does not say the angels appear, but that he sees them (8:1–2). They are the angels who stand always before God; traditionally they are thought to be the archangels, among whom are named Gabriel, Raphael and Michael. They represent all angels, ever in the presence of God. The opening of this scene is a piece of heavenly liturgy, beginning with silence, the silence of watchful prayer, of waiting on God. (So it should be in all churches, before the liturgy.) The angels are given trumpets; another angel comes forward with a censer (v. 3). The smoke of the incense arises 'with the prayers of the saints from the hand of the angel before God.' The trumpets would be especially significant to Jewish people, whose daily sacrifices were accompanied by trumpets, blown after the priest had offered incense on the golden altar within the temple. The priest entered the temple, while the people waited quietly outside. This is what was happening, in Luke's Gospel, when the priest Zechariah was visited by Gabriel. Then the trumpets were blown and the sacrifice proceeded.

After the sounding of the sixth trumpet the voice of another mighty angel is heard. There are several such in John's vision, whose voices are like thunder and whose presence commands the scene. This is one of the most memorable:

> Then I saw another mighty angel coming down from heaven, wrapped in a cloud, with a rainbow over his head, and his face was like the sun, and his legs like pillars of fire. He had a little scroll open in his hand. And he set his right foot on the sea, and his left foot on the land, and called out with a loud voice, like a lion roaring; when he called out the seven thunders sounded. And when the seven thunders had sounded, I was about to write, but I heard a voice from heaven saying, 'Seal up what the seven thunders have said, and do not write it down.' And the angel whom I saw standing on sea and land lifted up his right hand to heaven and swore by him who lives for ever and ever, who created heaven and what

is in it, the earth and what is in it, and the sea and what is in it, that there should be no more delay, but that in the days of the trumpet call to be sounded by the seventh angel, the mystery of God, as he announced to his servants the prophets, should be fulfilled. (10:1–7)

The great angel is a magnificent mediator and messenger. With his feet planted one on the land and one in the sea, and his right hand lifted to heaven, he brings together earth, seas and skies, and with the scroll gives the Word of God to the prophet (v. 9), once again linking him with Ezekiel. This is the 'angel of the covenant', standing for all God's dealings with his people, from the six days of creation until the final sounding of the seventh and last trumpet when every promise will be fulfilled.

Michael

If Michael is among the seven 'angels of the presence', then it is fitting that he should sound the seventh trumpet (11:15), after which he enters into battle, leading his angels against the evil forces. He is the commander of the Lord's army; he is the defender of the nation of Israel. The name 'Michael' means 'Who is like God?'; even in his commanding stature the whole being of the angel turns in deference to his God who is above all created being, all names. Christian tradition has placed Michael as the leader of all angels, giving his name to the annual feast-day, 29 September, that is kept in their honour.

The figure of Michael also forges links between this scene in the book of Revelation and the story of Joshua's capture of the city of Jericho (Josh. ch. 6) thus emphasizing the overall continuity of the history of salvation. God has set his people free, he guides them on their way, and has given them the protection of angels. Just before his miraculously successful assault on Jericho Joshua is greeted by an angel, 'the commander of the Lord's army' (see chapter. 1, Part I above). This angel could perhaps be identified with Michael, and seen as instrumental in Joshua's success. The next day Joshua commands seven priests with trumpets to go in front of those carrying the ark of the covenant. On six consecutive days they march six times round the city sounding the trumpets continuously. On the seventh day they circle the city seven times, and at the seventh time all the people following give a great shout, the walls of Jericho fall flat, and the Israelites march in, with the ark, to take the city. In Revelation the first six trumpets call forth destruction, tribulation and bloodshed. As the seventh trumpet is sounded, by Michael, loud voices proclaim the coming of the kingdom of God, a hymn is sung:

> Then God's temple in heaven was opened, and the ark of the covenant was seen within his temple; and there were flashes of lightning, voices, peals of thunder, an earthquake, and heavy hail. (Rev. 11:19)

The trumpets are the proclamation of final victory, though, as in the book of Joshua, there is more trouble to come. But the seven angels, and the call of their trumpets, are true apocalyptic signs of the parousia, to which John's book leads. The coming of the Son of Man in glory is the climax of creation, towards which everything is moving. At that moment of time, all will be transformed. The flesh and blood pictures in Revelation are intimations of that final transformation to immortality. Paul wrote:

> Just as we have borne the image of the man of dust, we shall bear the image of the man of heaven. I tell you this, brethren; flesh and blood cannot inherit the kingdom of God, nor does the perishable inherit the imperishable. Lo! I tell you a mystery. We shall not all sleep, but we shall all be changed, in a moment, in the twinkling of an eye, at the last trumpet. For the trumpet will sound, and the dead will be raised imperishable, and we shall be changed. (1 Cor. 15:49–52)

After the trumpets John sees the woman 'clothed with the sun' give birth to the child 'who is to rule all the nations';

Michael wages war with the dragon, 'that ancient serpent, who is called the Devil and Satan', who wanted to devour the child. The woman stands for Eve and Mary; the dragon connects the serpent of Genesis with Satan and all evil angels, so John sees the heavenly standing of Christ's mother threatened by satanic malice. Michael's battle with them represents the 'fall' of Satan and his followers; the last fall, in which rebel angels finally lose all claim to a place among the stars; and their fruitless struggles on and with the earth are portrayed (ch. 13). The faithful are meanwhile singing 'a new song', and John sees an angel flying between heaven and earth with the 'evangel', the good news. (This angel is the only one in John's vision to be described as flying.) Two more angels follow, proclaiming the fall of 'Babylon', and punishment for sin (14:6–13). The Christ-image of the son of man appears; he swings his sickle and his angel reapers fall to work at once. A climax is approaching, with the coming of another group of angels: 'seven angels with seven plagues, which are the last, for with them the wrath of God is ended' (15:1).

Other powerful angels appear

A climax is approaching. John describes, in melodramatic terms, how these angels pour out their seven golden bowls of the wrath of God upon the earth. The angels are 'robed in pure bright linen, and their breasts girded with golden girdles' (15:6). When the last bowl is poured a loud voice cries 'It is done' (16:17), and after a fearful storm one of the seven comes to John to explain the symbolism to him. 'Babylon' stands for all that is not of God in the world; illusory and transient pleasures, written in the burning language and imagery of John's day (ch. 17).

> After this I saw another angel coming down from heaven, having great authority; and the earth was made bright with his splendour. And he called out in a mighty voice: 'Fallen, fallen is Babylon the great!' (18:1–2)

Another 'mighty angel' appears; his strength serves him to hurl a millstone into the sea. The millstone may recall the 'large stones' of Jeremiah 43:9 which represent idolatry and sin. At once the great multitude of the heavenly host gives voice to a song of praise: 'Hallelujah! Salvation and glory and power belong to our God' (19:1). The whole pageant is alive and giving glory to God. John's angel, who has never left him, again commands him to 'Write this: Blessed are those who are invited to the marriage supper of the Lamb' (v. 9).

The vision is not over, there is another movement recapitulating much that has already passed before John's sight, preparing for the finale. The finale presents the eternal reality of heaven, seen as a holy city, the new Jerusalem, from which pours the river of life, as revealed to Ezekiel (22:1). John's angel, who also holds a measuring rod, shows him the city and the river and tells him that true worshippers shall worship there at the throne of God and the Lamb, and they shall see his face.

> And he said to me, 'These words are trustworthy and true, and the Lord the God of the spirits of the prophets has sent his angel to show his servants what must soon take place. And behold, I am coming very soon.' (22:6)

The angel has been guiding John towards the one and only truth, which is Christ. John falls at the angel's feet a second time, but is told once more:

> 'You must not do that! I am a fellow-servant with you and your brethren the prophets, and with those who keep the words of this book. Worship God.' . . . 'I Jesus have sent my angel to you with this testimony for the churches. I am the root and offspring of David, the bright morning star.' (22:9 and 16)

John writes:

He who testifies to these things says, 'Surely I am coming soon.' Amen. Come, Lord Jesus! (v. 20)

The angels of John's vision hold together the various parts of the dramatic revelation, particularly the different signs under which Christ appears in it. They guide John through, they direct all he writes, but nevertheless his writing must fail to communicate the whole meaning of what he saw; it was beyond his comprehension, and is beyond ours.

John wrote his apocalypse in the language of his time; he saw it in the images of his culture and traditions. These images will not speak to us in the same way, but the angels can continue their work of interpretation, if we look at the writing in the context of the Bible as a whole. We must never forget that Jesus was born into the tradition that produced John's writing. His teaching was largely given in the same idiom of number symbolism, vivid imagery and stylized language. 'You must forgive,' he said to Peter, 'not seven times, but seventy times seven' (Matt. 18:22). 'You who have followed me will also sit on twelve thrones, judging the twelve tribes of Israel' (Matt. 19:28). 'As the lightning flashes and lights up the sky from one side to the other, so will the Son of Man be in his day' (Luke 17:24). So the figure who stands before John and proclaims that the seven stars he holds in his hands are the seven angels of the churches is true to this aspect of the man Jesus Christ, as well as to his own promises that he will one day come again, in glory, with all his angels about him.

Notes for Part IV Chapter 4

[1] In this chapter I am indebted, from time to time, to A. Farrer, *The Revelation of St John the Divine* (O.U.P., Oxford, 1964). Those who wish to study Revelation in depth will find this commentary very useful.

[2] Farrer describes the vision as 'a celestial liturgy performed by Christ and his angels'. op.cit., p. 23.

5. Christ and his Angels

Why do you seek the living among the dead?
(LUKE 24:5)

Apocalyptic visions point to Christ, and the large part played by angels in them indicates the angels' importance in the Christian revelation. They are his angels, working in the world as essential constituents of creation, and their work assists in moving it towards its final perfection. In the Bible they are made visible, but from the accounts of their appearances we can learn much about the nature of their invisible activities, constantly performed throughout time. The apocalypses provide the key to the angels' motivation, in Christ, and the Gospels give account of several times when their service was made visible during his visible life on earth, as mediators, messengers and ministers.

On two occasions, in the Gospels, angels served Jesus in his need (Matt. 4:11 and Luke 22:43); we cannot know how many more there were that have not been revealed. His time of desolation and temptation in the wilderness, and his anguish in Gethsemane are precious gifts to us; the Gospel accounts offer insights into times when he was alone. To know that not only does he share our needs, but that his were so very great, is more than comfort; we can see his actual compassion for suffering humanity. The angels' presence exemplifies their ready assistance in all the pains of human life, as lived and suffered by Jesus, with us. They were there when he needed them, just as they are here for us, through him. Everything that we have discovered about angels in the course of this study tells of their nearness, their tight-knit relation to all creation of which they are an integral part, and most especially their activity in maintaining the bond between God and humankind, in Christ. This they do, not

226

only by speaking God's message, but by serving our needs in ways only to be acknowledged in faith, and by their power, which is beyond our comprehension, to mediate the power of God unfailingly.

Incarnation

The climax of all the work of angels, for all time, is their involvement in the beginning and ending of Jesus' life on earth.

> Glory to God in the highest, and on earth, peace among men. (Luke 2:14)

So sang the company of angels, heard only by a few shepherds, at the moment when heaven and earth were truly joined for the first time, in the fullness of time. The message had been given by angels, by Gabriel to Mary, and in an angel-dream to Joseph. At the birth in Bethlehem the 'multitude of the heavenly host' allowed their song of praise to be heard, and instructed a few poor people to go and worship also.

Why only those few? Why, when the doors of heaven opened, and the brilliant light of eternity became visible from dark earth, were there not more people to see it, and why was the glimpse so brief? These questions could be asked about all the momentary 'sights' of heaven – the door opens and a light shines from eternity into time. A glimpse of heaven is granted; and, more, the earth is lit up by divine light, and for that moment participates in eternity. The point is made by Annie Dillard, writing in America. She saw a cedar tree lit by the setting sun, which made her feel for a moment 'more alive than all the world':

> I had thought, because I had seen the tree with the lights in it, that the great door, by definition, opens on eternity. Now . . .I discover that . . . it nevertheless opened on the real and present cedar. It opened on time: Where else?

That Christ's incarnation occurred improbably, ridiculously, at such-and-such a time, into such-and-such a place, is referred to – with great sincerity even among believers – as 'the scandal of particularity'. Well, the 'scandal of particularity' is the only world that I, in particular, know. What use has eternity for light? We're all up to our necks in this particular scandal . . . I never saw a tree that was no tree in particular.[1]

Angels appear at particular moments to particular people; when this happens, that place and time share in eternity. In Christ God came to earth at a particular moment, in order to show that he is with us at every moment. Angels become visible at particular moments and show that they are at work in every moment. Their function is first to bring heaven to us so that they may bring us to heaven.

Resurrection

The biblical narrative describes how angels announced the conception and birth of Jesus, but nothing is told of their work in these silent mysteries that Mary kept, and pondered in her heart. It is the same with his death and resurrection, the highest moment of all, in the silent tomb. No words can frame the exultation of this mystery of mysteries, in which the angels surely would have taken part. The Gospels again give account of how the angels delivered the message that Christ had risen, and the narratives vary in dramatic intensity. The variations display different aspects of angelic activity.

John records only that two men in white, whom Mary Magdalene saw when she looked into the tomb after Peter and John had gone, said gently to her, 'Woman, why are you weeping?' They turned her towards Jesus, even as she turned away from them; he was standing outside the tomb. He repeated the words his angels had just spoken. Their courtesy is reminiscent of Gabriel's demeanour to Daniel (John 20:12–15).

In Luke the angels asked Mary and the women with her, 'Why do you seek the living among the dead?' (Luke 24:5). This question should be addressed again and again, by all of us, and most searchingly by those in authority in the Church. It is too easy to see the traditions of Christian faith and practice as fixed; to try and find the living Christ only in static images, rather than in each particular moment of life. The same can be said for his angels: we should not look at angels only in terms of texts and pictures; they are among the living. The Bible text can be alive, in the Holy Spirit, if we recognize its power as it sheds light on this present time, where its angels are always at work. 'Remember how he told you,' the angels at the tomb continued, 'while he was still in Galilee, that the Son of Man must be delivered into the hands of sinful men, and be crucified, and on the third day, rise' (Luke 24:6–7). The angels will remind us of all that Christ has said, about himself, and the Father, through the Holy Spirit. These reminders will come through the liturgy, first of all, and in prayer, reading and thought, whenever our minds are open to receive them. Such openness may also serve to open our eyes – we may indeed see angels.

Mark tells how an angel pointed out the place where the body of Jesus had lain, and instructed the women to go and tell the disciples; they were to be the messengers of this great event (Mark 16:6–7). Matthew's text draws all the accounts together:

Now after the sabbath, toward the dawn of the first day of the week, Mary Magdalene and the other Mary went to see the sepulchre. And behold, there was a great earthquake; for an angel of the Lord descended from heaven and came and rolled back the stone, and sat upon it. His appearance was like lightning, and his raiment white as snow. And for fear of him the guards trembled and became like dead men. But the angel said to the women, 'Do not be afraid; for I know that you seek Jesus who was crucified. He is not here; for he has risen, as he said. Come, see the place where he lay. Then go quickly and tell his disciples that he has risen from the dead, and behold, he is going before you to Galilee; there you will see him. Lo, I have told you.' (Matt. 28:1–8)

'Lo, I have told you': the angels' mission. 'I am Gabriel, who stand in the presence of God; and I was sent to speak to you, and to bring this good news' (Luke 1:19). The angels speak the gospel, and they act in its events. Matthew has an angel roll away the stone; his entry marked by an earthquake, and his appearance like lightning. An angel shone the light of eternity that morning, into that garden, leaving no doubt as to the cosmic significance of the happening there.

Ascension

Angels were also in action for the removal from earth of the visible presence of the risen Jesus. Two of them were made visible, as soon as he had ascended, and they said to his disciples, 'Men of Galilee, why do you stand looking into heaven? This Jesus, who was taken up from you into heaven, will come in the same way as you saw him go into heaven' (Acts 1:11). Rather than the withdrawal of Jesus, the disciples are seeing an apocalyptic vision, after the manner of Daniel's sight of the 'son of man', but the most important message which is endorsed by the presence of the angels, is Jesus' promise: 'Lo, I am with you always . . .' Ikon paintings of the ascension of Christ underline this, with their depiction of the angels mingled with the crowd of disciples, including Mary the mother of Christ. There is an intimacy of association; the angels always with us and among us, in communal adoration of Christ.

A tradition among the Fathers of the Church holds that the angels assisted in the ascension (as they assisted in all the events of Christ's human life), carrying him 'up', accompanying him, and calling for the gates to open: 'Lift up your heads, O gates . . . that the King of Glory may come in!' (Ps. 24:7 and 9).[2] Medieval mystery plays of the ascension have welcoming angels cry out from heaven, in words from

Isaiah, 'Who is this who comes from Edom, in crimsoned garments . . . ?' (Isa. 63:1).[3] In Acts we read that 'he was lifted up . . . out of their sight', giving rise to the idea that the angels lifted him. More important is the lifting up, or exaltation, of human nature which the Word of God united to himself, above the order of angels. The angels assisted, and rejoiced, in his descent to manhood; now they rejoice and welcome humanity to a place superior to theirs. They, spirits who are free from the power of death, and thus higher than we are in the order of creation, exist for the purpose of guiding us, and the whole universe, into our proper places, which for human beings is above them. Paul wrote: 'Do you not know that we are to judge angels?' (1 Cor. 6:3), describing our ultimate ascendancy.

Christ and his angels in Hebrews

The letter to the Hebrews sets out a theology of angels in its first two chapters, interwoven with the Christology to which it is subject. The Son of God 'reflects the glory of God and bears the very stamp of his nature, upholding the universe by his word of power' (1:3). 'Let all God's angels worship him . . . who makes his angels winds, and his servant's flames of fire . . . sent forth to serve, for the sake of those who are to obtain salvation' (vv. 6, 7 and 14). We, 'the descendants of Abraham' (2:16) (that means the *whole* human race), as children of God are called to be Christ's equals; 'for he who sanctifies, and those who are sanctified have all one origin' (2:11). We too can reflect the glory of God, and bear the very stamp of his nature, and have the angels 'under our feet', but we cannot actually see this yet. While we are journeying here on earth the angels still appear to be superior to us, in nature and power.

But we see Jesus, who for a little while was made lower than the angels, crowned with glory and honour because of the suffering of death, so that by the grace of God he might taste death for everyone. For it was

231

fitting that he for whom and by whom all things exist, in bringing many children to glory, should make the pioneer of their salvation perfect through suffering. (Heb. 2:9–10)

All the work of angels is nothing, would be of no avail at all, without the death of Christ. Their ministry serves, outside time, the insertion into history of the incarnation which gathered up the angels' mortal charges and raised us all to our destined immortal status. Only the descent of Christ into mortality could accomplish this. Through death he would destroy death. The forces of evil have fought against the inevitability of the victory of God, and will continue to fight, so it seems, while time lasts. But the angels of God willingly help to bring about the reversal of their status and ours, exemplified by the Son of God. We have seen how they ministered to him in his suffering human life, through which we receive help: 'for because he himself has suffered and been tempted he is able to help those who are tempted' (2:18). Their service to him is also their service to us in him. And in him the angels find, as we do, the complete fulfilment of their nature and being.

To be aware of the nature and being of angels is to enter into 'the higher dream'. We are not bound by material limitations, by what we can see, touch, and measure here on earth; we have entrance to the invisible, an inner ear to hear and understand 'the token of the word unheard, unspoken'. When our eyes are opened the angels' light can illumine the present moment. In the texts, they present symbols: fire and water, as signs of the Holy Spirit; they appear as men, with a courteous demeanour to manifest the love of God; they exert power (which at times seems adverse), give light, and display supernatural movement, to denote their divine motivation. These images are a necessary part of our understanding of them; they can lead us to find the angels themselves. Being with the angels here and now, we are brought to where we and they belong:

For you have not come to what may be touched, a blazing fire, and darkness, and gloom, and a tempest, and the sound of a trumpet . . . you have come to Mount Zion and to the city of the living God, the heavenly Jerusalem, and to the innumerable angels in festal gathering, . . . and to Jesus the mediator of a new covenant. (Heb. 12:18–19, 22 and 24)

The angels of God the Father, Son and Holy Spirit

The angels lead us to Christ, and in him we shall most truly find them. As we are promised his presence with us at all times, here on earth, so the angels are all about us, every day, in, through and with him, but we should never take them for granted; they are holy. We may discover for ourselves the paradox Jacob experiences at Bethel: both the awesomeness and the reassurance of divine presence. We cannot see God face to face and live, yet in Christ God is nearer to each of us than we are to ourselves. Christ has his own ineffable majesty, before whom 'every knee should bow, in heaven and on earth and under the earth' (Phil. 2:10), and his angels would overcome us totally were they to appear before us in all their power; even so, he himself, and the angels, come down to us in our lowest need. Time after time, in the Bible, the angel's first words to a trembling hearer are 'Fear not . . .' The twentieth-century German poet R. M. Rilke, though he distanced himself from Christian faith, reminds us, in one of his most famous poems, that 'every angel is terrible' (*'Jeder Engel ist schrecklich'*). Gone now, in this image, is the simple companionship offered to Tobias by the angel; Rilke scarcely dares to invoke it:

Träte der Erzengel jetzt, der gefährliche, hinter den Sternen
eines Schrittes nur nieder und herwärts: hochauf-

233

schlagend erschlüg uns das eigene Herz.
Wer seid ihr?

(Let the archangel dangerous now, from behind the
stars
step but a step down hitherwards: high up-beating,
our heart would out-beat us.
Who are you?)

You are, the poet suggests:

Höhenzüge, morgenrötliche Grate
aller Erschaffung, – Pollen der blühenden Gottheit

(Ranges, summits, dawn-red ridges
of all forthbringing – pollen of blossoming godhead.)

To Rilke the grandeur and creativity of these angel-beings is
far removed from human life and endeavour, and their power
and mystery not only unfathomable, but alien, even inimical
to humankind. A few lines later Rilke sees the angels,
suddenly, as separate mirrors, but instead of reflecting the
light of God, as in the Dionysian system, they reflect only
themselves, taking their 'outstreamed beauty' back into their
own faces; they do not relate to anything outside their own
brilliance, and might even absorb the transient essence of
humanity. Rilke's poems contain unforgettable images of the
fearful transcendence of angels, but in Judaeo-Christian
writings the angels' world of light illumines our world, and
our world shares in theirs. There is concourse between
heaven and earth; the purpose of this concourse, we believe,
is to raise the visible world to the invisible, where they will
be united, in God. The book of Job presents the Divine as
beyond human comprehension, but there Job hears the voice
of God in the whirlwind, and in this communication he finds
peace, not because he then understands the mystery of God,
but because God has addressed him. God addresses us out of
divine sovereignty, but also in simplicity, and he addresses

us through angels. The angels often manifest such extremes as are found on the one hand in the great angels of the book of Revelation and on the other in the story of Elijah, who is awakened by an angel offering him water and a fresh-baked scone.

Everyone who has tried to pray knows the extremes of experience encountered along the way. Most of us will meet with some sort of struggle in the nature of Jacob's wrestling with the angel of God. Thomas Merton writes:

> I have prayed to You in the day-time with thoughts and reasons, and in the night-time You have confronted me, scattering thought and reason. I have come to You in the morning with light and desire, and You have descended on me, with great gentleness, with most forbearing silence, in this inexplicable night, dispersing light, defeating all desire . . . While I am asking questions You do not answer, You ask me a question which is so simple that I cannot answer.[5]

If we desire to know God and his angels we must continue to enquire, but, as with Jacob, the one question in the end is 'What is your name?' The name, or essence, of every angel originates in its participation in the Holy Name of God. We have begun to understand this through studying the revelations of angelic activity, as found in the Bible, and may continue through our own experience and that of others. The Church's liturgy can and should open us to the reality of the angels' worship of God, and so enrich and vitalize our own worship. Faith will lead us further into a personal acceptance of the angels' assistance, in prayer and all areas of daily life. Then, just as prayer may be deepened by the letting go of images, our trust in angelic power will also be stronger if we relinquish dependence on visible symbols. The angels will themselves assist us to live and move in the Spirit, as they live and move.

Christians must be constantly attuned to the Holy Spirit. There are signs that many people today are newly aware of this. Social issues will always demand the attention of Christians, but true peace and justice can flow only from God, so the more we seek the spiritual dimension of human life, the more we shall move towards a properly ordered humanity, as the Holy Spirit works through us, in union with the angels. The only thing that can bring this about is prayer, and ultimately the power of angels will be most effective, for us and for the world, in the silence of faith and the contemplation of God the Holy Trinity.

Notes for Part IV Chapter 5

[1] Annie Dillard, *Pilgrim at Tinker Creek* (Pan Books, London, 1976) p. 79.
[2] See J. Daniélou, *Les Anges et leur Mission* (Belgium, 1953).
[3] Chester Cycle, in P. Happé ed, *English Mystery Plays* (Harmondsworth, Penguin, 1975). In the play the angels speak the text in the Latin of the Vulgate, to which the audience would be accustomed: *'Quis est iste qui venit de Edom, tinctis vestibus de Bosra?'*
[4] R. M. Rilke, *Duino Elegies* 2, trans. J. B. Leishman and S. Spender (Hogarth Press, London, 1968).
[5] Thomas Merton, *The Sign of Jonas* (Hollis and Carter, London, 1953) pp. 344–5 and 347.)

Index